Jussara Pretti Korngold

THE PRISM OF GRIEF

Love, Loss, and Awakening Across the Seasons of Life

Jussara Pretti Korngold

THE PRISM OF GRIEF

Love, Loss, and Awakening Across the Seasons of Life

The Prism of Grief: Love, Loss, and Awakening Across the Seasons of Life

Published by: United States Spiritist Council
ISBN: 978-1-948109-49-9
LCCN: 2026937987
Credits:
Cover Design and Interior Layout: Diego Henrique e Jussara Korngold

First Edition: 2026 Printed in the United States of America

Dedication

To those who loved and lost,
and discovered that love does not end with absence.
To those who grieve in silence.
May these pages remind you that grief is not the end of love,
but one of its deepest languages.
"The prism does not fracture the light. It reveals what the light already contains."

Table of Contents

Preface

The Prism

We often speak of grief in the singular, as though it were a single weight to be carried or a solitary hurdle to be overcome. Yet anyone who has walked through the terrain of real loss knows that grief is never one thing. It shifts in tone. It changes temperature. It reveals different faces depending on what was lost and who we were when it happened. Grief is plural—a slow refraction of the self.

The image that best expresses this complexity is the prism.

A prism receives a beam of white light and refracts it into a spectrum of color. The light itself is not broken or diminished; it is revealed. What was always contained within it becomes visible only when it passes through resistance.

Loss does not create love; it reveals it. When love encounters the resistance of separation, it refracts into longing, sorrow, anger, fear, memory, gratitude, and eventually compassion. None of these colors is accidental. Each is a facet through which consciousness learns to deepen.

This book follows grief through its prism-like unfolding. It begins in the visible spectrum—in the colors of childhood, adolescence, adulthood, and maturity, and in the losses that accompany health, identity, beauty, and status. It then moves beyond color into structure—into the thread that binds us, the veil that confronts us, and the labyrinth that turns us inward. Finally, it reaches the elements—fire that purifies, gold that refines, and the reintegrated light that returns not as naïveté, but as maturity.

The prism does not promise the absence of darkness. It reveals that even when light appears fractured, it remains light. May these pages help you recognize your own colors within loss—and discover that what has been refracted has not been destroyed.

Introduction

On Learning to See Through the Prism

This book was not born from theory alone. It emerged from decades of listening, studying, observing, stumbling, and returning — again and again — to the questions life refuses to let us ignore: loss, suffering, impermanence, love, death, and the meaning we assign to what cannot be avoided.

For over thirty years, I have had the privilege of learning from two luminous figures in the field of spiritual psychology and Spiritist thought: Joanna de Ângelis and Divaldo Pereira Franco[1]. Their works shaped not only my intellectual understanding of grief and inner transformation, but my way of inhabiting life. More than concepts, they offered a lens. More than answers, they provided a method — one grounded in ethical responsibility, psychological lucidity, and compassion for the human condition.

I do not write from authority, but from apprenticeship. I write as one who continues to learn by living—by witnessing suffering in myself and others, and by recognizing that the most unavoidable themes of life are also the most transformative. This work approaches grief not as pathology or punishment, but as a movement of consciousness. What appears

1 To learn more about the lives and extensive humanitarian and literary works of Joanna de Ângelis and Divaldo Franco, visit Mansão do Caminho (https://mansaodocaminho.com.br) or explore their translated psychological series at Leal Publisher (https://lealpublisher.com).

fragmented in loss may, in time, reveal an unsuspected coherence.

The journey traced in these pages does not move in a straight line. It unfolds, deepens, and returns. What initially seems like rupture may eventually reorganize the interior landscape, allowing the soul to find its own Luminous Coherence.

The intention here is not to teach grief from above, but to reflect upon it from within. These pages are offered as companionship in crossing—a shared inquiry into how rupture reorganizes meaning, how love survives change of form, and how suffering, when listened to rather than silenced, becomes a school for consciousness.

While these chapters are organized by life stages and specific facets of loss, they are meant to be used as a resource. You may find yourself drawn to the Blue Facet of childhood shadows or the Silver Facet of aging. You are invited to walk these pages patiently, at your own pace, recognizing that we are not meant to bypass loss; we are meant to pass through it—slowly, imperfectly, and humanly.

What feels like ending may reveal itself as transformation. What seems at first to be the breaking of light may ultimately become the way light learns to shine with greater depth.

Jussara Pretti Korngold
New York, 2026

Chapter 1 | The Prism

A Refraction of the Soul

Grief is the first place where the soul learns that love can remain even when presence disappears.

Often imagined as something that belongs only to later seasons of life, sorrow is mistakenly confined to adulthood—as though grief required years of accumulation before it could enter the human story. Yet it does not wait for time to authorize its arrival. It enters the human experience the moment attachment is born. To love is already to expose oneself to the possibility of absence. Even before the intellect can name what has been lost, the heart begins to feel the tremor of separation.

More than an emotional reaction to death, grief is a fundamental experience of rupture—the moment when continuity is interrupted. The soul, accustomed to bonds, suddenly encounters the boundary of form.

The Prism of Grief

Something that was present becomes absent. Something that was embodied withdraws from the field of the senses. What breaks is not only a relationship, but a structure of meaning. The world that included a certain face, a certain voice, a certain daily rhythm no longer exists in the same way. The familiar landscape is altered.

To contain such complexity, the image of the prism becomes especially illuminating. A prism receives a single beam of white light. It does not fracture the light, nor weaken it. Instead, it reveals what the light already contains—colors, layers, and depths previously invisible to the eye. What appeared singular becomes plural. What seemed whole discloses unsuspected nuance.

As the prism turns, grief becomes not only loss, but a language through which the soul slowly learns to see itself.

This rupture is not merely emotional; it is biological and neurological. Contemporary research shows that intense mourning activates pain circuits in the brain, attachment systems similar to addiction, and stress responses that affect immunity and cardiovascular health. This is why early grief often feels like withdrawal: the body is relearning how to exist without a regulating presence woven into its rhythms. Love leaves fingerprints on the nervous system. When love is interrupted, the entire organism must reorganize itself—not only psychologically, but physiologically. Grief is, therefore, the body and soul learning to inhabit absence.

It begins in the nervous system, yet it does not remain there. What starts as biological shock gradually unfolds into questions of meaning, identity, and continuity.

More than emotion is unsettled in loss. Identity, perception, and coherence themselves are shaken. What once offered orientation dissolves into uncertainty. The world feels less reliable, less predictable, less whole. Invisible architecture—those assumptions that quietly sustained everyday life—trembles. One may still move through the same rooms, speak to the same people, follow familiar routines, yet something essential has shifted beneath the surface. Reality feels subtly foreign, as though one were inhabiting a version of the world that no longer fully belongs to the self that existed before the loss.

In cultures that prize productivity, restraint, and efficiency, grief is often mistaken for weakness. Mourning may be interpreted as a failure of resilience or self-control. Yet sorrow is not the absence of strength—it is evidence of love. Where there was no bond, there can be no mourning. Pain is not a flaw in the human condition; it is the imprint of connection.

Beyond emotional pain lies existential suffering. Psychological grief reflects the ache of absence, the yearning for what is no longer present. The ancient Greeks named this experience *póthos*: the pain of the absence of a presence—a longing born not of emptiness, but of love. Existential suffering arises when loss dismantles meaning itself, when grief asks not only *How do I live without this?* but also *Who am I now?* and *What does life require of me?*

From a psychological perspective, grief is not a single emotion but a constellation: sadness, anger, fear, guilt, relief, longing, confusion, and sometimes even peace. These emotions do not unfold in orderly sequence. They coexist, overlap, contradict one another, and appear without warning. Many believe they are grieving "incorrectly" because their inner experience feels chaotic. In truth, this disorganization reflects the loosening of previous structures of identity. What is lost is not only a person or relationship, but roles, certainties, future projections, and the narrative one told oneself about who one was in the world.

Yet this loosening is not meaningless. Carl Jung observed that before psychic transformation occurs, the ego's previous organization often softens or collapses. What feels like chaos may be threshold. The psyche must release what it believed itself to be in order to become what it has not yet learned to be. Grief initiates this process not by preference, but by necessity. It confronts consciousness with limits it would rather avoid: impermanence, vulnerability, and the impossibility of preserving love through control.

What psychology describes as reorganization, mythology narrates as descent.

Joseph Campbell, a great interpreter of myth and of the initiatory paths of human experience, observed that the hero's journey rarely begins with triumph. It begins with rupture—with exile, loss, and the disruption of ordinary life. In this sense, grief is one of the most universal calls to transformation. It pushes the soul beyond familiar territories into landscapes it did not choose. Whether welcomed or resisted, the descent has already begun. The old world no longer holds. A threshold has been crossed.

Few myths portray this descent as vividly as the story of Orpheus. When Eurydice dies, Orpheus descends into the underworld seeking to retrieve what was lost. His impulse is unmistakably human: when grief strikes, we long to reverse reality itself. We wish to undo the irrevocable. We imagine that if we descend far enough into sorrow or memory, we might bring the beloved back into form. Orpheus is granted a conditional return—Eurydice may follow him back, provided he does not turn to look at her before reaching the surface. The condition reveals the psychological essence of grief: movement without reassurance, trust without visible confirmation. Unable to bear uncertainty, he turns. She disappears again. The myth does not condemn him; it illuminates the struggle inherent in transition. Orpheus returns transformed—not because he retrieved what was lost, but because he confronted absence directly. So too with grief: we descend hoping to recover what was taken, yet we emerge altered instead.

A complementary vision appears in the myth of Demeter and Persephone. When Persephone is taken into the underworld, Demeter's sorrow becomes cosmic. She withdraws vitality from the earth itself. Crops fail. Winter spreads. Life mirrors inner barrenness. Yet the myth refuses permanence of despair. A rhythm is restored. Persephone belongs to two realms—part of the year above ground, part below. Life resumes, though forever changed. The lesson is compassionate: after profound loss, we often inhabit two worlds simultaneously. Part of us returns to daily life; part remains with what was lost. Healing does not erase winter—it restores rhythm.

Where myth speaks in symbol, philosophy seeks coherence.

From a Spiritist perspective, that coherence deepens further. In the works of Allan Kardec—the 19th-century educator and researcher who systematized

Spiritism as a philosophical, scientific, and ethical framework—the human being is understood as an immortal soul temporarily experiencing physical existence. Death, therefore, is not annihilation, though it constitutes a real separation in form and presence. Spiritual knowledge does not erase grief; it reframes it. Love does not end with death, nor does longing. The persistence of yearning is not a failure of faith, but testimony to continuity of bonds.

From a Spiritist psychological perspective, Joanna de Ângelis observes that life's experiences do not create the essence of the being; rather, they reveal latent contents of the spirit. The circumstances of existence function as catalysts, bringing to the surface what is already inscribed in the deeper layers of consciousness.

The soul carries ancient experiences, while personality gradually unfolds within the conditions of earthly life. When loss occurs—especially in early childhood—it may crystallize into abandonment anxiety, excessive control, or emotional numbing if it is dismissed or silenced.

When accompanied by presence, by truth adapted to each person's capacity for understanding, and by emotional shelter, the experience of loss can cultivate resilience, empathy, and moral sensitivity. What ultimately shapes the future is not loss alone, but how it is interpreted, named, and held within a loving presence.

Such a perspective also cautions against spiritual bypassing—the attempt to silence emotional truth with metaphysical explanation. Mourning must be lived, not denied. Spiritual understanding does not cancel grief; it provides horizon.

It is neither illusion nor punishment. It is invitation.

Grief asks something precise of the soul. It asks us to stop bargaining with reality and allow the loss to be real. It asks love to evolve—to accept that love does not disappear, but changes form. It asks identity to loosen and reform, acknowledging that we are not only what we lost, yet we are no longer who we were before. Above all, it asks us to honor time—not as enemy to be conquered, but as ally in the slow maturation of consciousness.

Carried alone, grief may harden into fear of attachment, distrust of continuity, or the quiet belief that loving deeply is dangerous. Accompanied by presence and truth, it becomes the place where the heart learns to love without demanding permanence. Loss does not take love away; it reveals how deeply love was already rooted. What disappears is the illusion that love can be protected from vulnerability. What remains is the discovery that love, once awakened, does not belong only to form.

The prism does not fracture light but reveals what light already contains. In the same way, grief does not destroy love; it discloses its depth, its vulnerability, and its capacity to transcend form. What appears as rupture may be the first revelation of deeper continuity—when love begins to exist beyond what can be held.

Yet this lesson is not first learned in adulthood. Its earliest tremors are felt much sooner, within the fragile architecture of childhood, where protection seems eternal and absence feels incomprehensible.

The Prism of Grief

It is there—in the blue light of early attachment—that grief first introduces the soul to vulnerability.

Long before language.

Long before philosophy.

Long before the mind can explain what the heart already knows.

And it is there, in that first encounter with absence, that the prism of grief begins to turn.

Chapter 2 | The Blue Facet

Shadows in the Playground

The prism opens in blue.

The first color to emerge is the grief of childhood—the loss of safety and unquestioned belonging.

Here the soul first learns vulnerability.

Childhood is the first place where the soul discovers that protection is not permanent—and that love, when it can no longer shelter, begins to teach.

Often imagined as a sanctuary untouched by loss, childhood is romanticized as a season of innocence, play, and protected joy. Adults speak of it as though sorrow belonged elsewhere—reserved for later years, for those equipped to understand impermanence. Yet grief does not wait for maturity. It arrives early, sometimes quietly, sometimes violently. When it enters childhood, it rarely appears as philosophical reflection. It manifests as fear of being left behind, confusion before absence, rupture of safety, and the dawning realization that the world is not entirely predictable.

The blue facet of grief carries the tones of attachment, trust, emotional bonding, and vulnerability. Blue is the color of safety felt in another's presence—the quiet assurance that someone stronger is near, that the world is held together by dependable arms. When loss touches this landscape, it does not merely remove a person or circumstance; it alters the child's perception of reality itself. What once felt stable becomes uncertain. What seemed eternal reveals its fragility. Childhood grief is therefore not only about losing someone; it is also the loss of the illusion that protection is permanent.

Children do not grieve with the linear logic of adults. Their inner world is symbolic, imaginal, relational. When loss occurs, the child rarely formulates existential questions about finitude. Instead, the questions are intimate and frightening:

Did I cause this?

Will this happen to me?

Will everyone leave?

This mode of thinking—often described as *magical thinking*—is not pathology. It is the natural language of a developing psyche. The child experiences the world as animated by intention and causality. When grief enters this symbolic field, guilt may arise—not because wrongdoing occurred, but because the child feels inwardly responsible for what happens around them.

For this reason, grief often migrates into the body. A child may not say, *I am grieving*, yet grief speaks through stomachaches, headaches, night terrors, bed-wetting, regressions, irritability, withdrawal, or sudden fears. The body becomes language when words are insufficient. What cannot yet be symbolized seeks somatic expression.

Contemporary science confirms that this bodily response is not metaphorical. The brain of a child is highly plastic and deeply dependent on *co-regulation*—the process by which an adult's steady presence stabilizes the child's nervous system. When a primary attachment is disrupted, the loss is experienced not only emotionally but physiologically. Brain imaging studies reveal that grief activates pain centers similar to physical injury, alongside attachment circuits and stress systems. Love leaves imprints on the nervous system from the beginning of life. When that regulating presence disappears, the body must relearn how to organize itself. The playground becomes a stage where laughter and sorrow coexist, and adults—seeing only behavior—may misinterpret these signals as defiance or distraction. Yet beneath the surface, the child is learning that absence exists.

Childhood grief often appears in two distinct forms.

The first is the concrete loss of others: the death of a loved one, parental separation, relocation, illness, addiction, or emotional withdrawal. These ruptures fracture continuity. The child's world—structured around dependable figures—shifts abruptly.

The second loss is more subtle and often overlooked: the loss of childhood itself. Growing out of childhood is also a form of mourning. The child must relinquish a world governed by immediacy, imagination, and dependency in order to enter a reality shaped by differentiation and responsibility. This passage is not neutral. It is a symbolic death of innocence. When favorite games lose enchantment and the body begins to change, the child senses—without words—that something irreversible has begun. A door closes quietly behind them.

From a broader spiritual perspective, this vulnerability is not accidental. Human beings enter life dependent, impressionable, and deeply open to the experiences that shape their sensitivity. Childhood is therefore a season of exposure and learning. When grief enters during this period, it reaches a psyche that is still forming its most fundamental relationship with trust. The wound concerns not only what was lost; it also touches how the child understands the continuity of life itself.

From a Spiritist psychological perspective, reflections found in the works of Joanna de Ângelis suggest that what shapes the future is not loss itself, but the way it is interpreted and held. When grief is denied or silenced, it may crystallize into abandonment anxiety, excessive control, or emotional numbing. When, however, loss is accompanied by presence, language adapted to the child's capacity, and emotional shelter, it can cultivate resilience, empathy, and early moral sensitivity. What shapes the future is not loss alone, but how it is interpreted and held.

Silence surrounding death often intensifies fear. The instinct for self-preservation makes death appear threatening, but when adults avoid naming it, imagination fills the void with shadows. Fairy tales, monsters, abandonment fantasies, and catastrophic images arise from the unconscious when truth is withheld. When death is presented gently—as part of life's rhythm rather than a forbidden catastrophe—the child is spared the burden of terror without explanation. Awareness of continuity need not be imposed in abstract terms; it may simply live within family language as reassurance: love does not end with separation, and bonds are not erased by absence.

Mythology understands this terrain deeply. Fairy tales, often dismissed as childish fantasy, are symbolic maps of early encounters with loss. Few illustrate this as vividly as Hansel and Gretel. Beneath its simplicity lies archetypal grief: the loss of protection.

The forest represents the collapse of security. Psychologically, it mirrors disorientation. Hansel's stones and breadcrumbs symbolize the child's attempt to control loss—to recreate the path back to safety. Children who experience grief often cling to rituals, objects, or exaggerated compliance, hoping to prevent further rupture. At first, the stones succeed. Later, the breadcrumbs vanish. This moment marks the encounter with irreversibility. Some losses cannot be undone.

The gingerbread house represents false refuge—sweetness without safety. In later life, unresolved childhood grief may repeat this pattern through substitutes: compulsive relationships, addictions, emotional dependence. The witch symbolizes the danger of confusing comfort with care. Discernment is born here.

Gretel's act of confronting the witch symbolizes the emergence of autonomy. Grief forces development. Through loss, resources awaken: courage, cooperation, and moral initiative. The children do not return unchanged. Healing does not restore innocence; it transforms it.

Ultimately, childhood grief introduces the soul to separation. It teaches that love changes form, that protection may falter, and that meaning must sometimes be rebuilt. The blue facet does not end in the playground. It quietly shapes future seasons—how trust is offered, how vulnerability is carried.

When childhood grief is endured alone, it may become the silent architecture of adult fear. When accompanied with truth and tenderness, it becomes the foundation of depth and empathy.

Childhood grief does not destroy the soul's capacity to trust. It reveals how trust was once dependent on external protection, so that, over time, trust may take root within. What appears at first as the loss of shelter may later become the first awakening of inner support.

Yet childhood is not the final terrain of vulnerability. As the blue tenderness of early attachment gives way to the heat of becoming, grief does not soften—it intensifies. Protection recedes. Desire awakens. And the soul, no longer sheltered by innocence, must learn to remain steady within its own rising intensity.

Chapter 3 | The Red Facet

Adolescence and the Storms of the Soul

The prism ignites in red.

Adolescence confronts the soul with a new grief—the grief of identity and desire.

Here the self struggles to be born.

Adolescence is the threshold where the soul first touches fire—and must learn that intensity is not the same as truth.

If childhood grief is blue—tender, dependent, shaped by the loss of protection—adolescence burns red.

This season does not whisper; it ignites. It arrives with heat, urgency, rebellion, and contradiction. The adolescent grieves not only those who are lost, but the very self that is dissolving. The child-self fades, and no stable adult-self has yet emerged. Between what is dying and what has not yet been born, the young soul inhabits a dangerous in-between.

Loss during adolescence unfolds in layers. There is the sorrow of leaving childhood behind, now felt more acutely as the body changes, desire awakens, and the world demands differentiation. There is the disillusionment of discovering that parents are fallible, institutions imperfect, and the world unjust. There is the pain of fractured friendships—through distance, betrayal, drugs, or suicide. And there is the deeper anguish of losing certainty about identity itself: *Who am I? Who am I allowed to be? Who will love me if I become who I truly am?*

In this landscape, grief often disguises itself. It appears as anger, defiance, withdrawal, sarcasm, excess, or numbness. Adolescents rarely say *I am grieving*. Instead they say *I don't care, Leave me alone,* or *Nothing matters.* The red facet burns because love is awakening in new forms—romantic longing, erotic curiosity, and a thirst for recognition—while protection is receding. The soul wants to fly, yet its wings are still fragile.

Sexuality enters this terrain not only as discovery, but as exposure. Desire reveals vulnerability. To desire is to risk being seen—and therefore rejected. For many, this risk feels unbearable. The body becomes a site of shame, confusion, or performance. Questions of sexual identity, orientation, and belonging emerge precisely when the psyche is least stable. What should be a sacred unfolding can become a battlefield between inner truth and external expectation.

At the same time, the influence of media intensifies fragmentation. The adolescent is no longer formed only by family and immediate community, but by screens, algorithms, curated images of perfection, hypersexualized bodies, and relentless comparison. Adolescents—still emotionally unstructured—are particularly vulnerable to seductive social models that promise pleasure, recognition, and belonging without demanding inner maturity. The image begins to eclipse the being. The persona is sculpted not for authenticity, but for survival.

Bullying—whether in school corridors or digital arenas—deepens this fracture. To survive ridicule, many adolescents begin to bury aspects of themselves. They learn to disappear inwardly in order to appear outwardly acceptable. They edit their truth. They silence their spontaneity. This is a subtle death: authenticity exchanged for conditional belonging. Here, grief is not only about losing others, but about losing oneself in order to remain included.

The myth of Icarus illuminates this storm of longing. Icarus is not merely reckless; he is intoxicated by possibility. He is hungry for the sun. Adolescence is Icarian by nature: desire awakens before discernment matures. The wings—sexuality, imagination, ideals, rebellion—are real, yet fragile. When the adolescent flies too close to the sun of absolute freedom, total pleasure, or radical self-definition without grounding, the fall can be devastating. The myth does not condemn aspiration; it reveals the necessity of balance between fire and measure, intensity and integration.

Drugs enter this landscape as artificial wings. They promise flight without effort, intensity without meaning, belonging without vulnerability. When adolescents, overwhelmed by inner conflict and lacking emotional scaffolding, seek refuge in drugs or excess, they are not pursuing pleasure alone—they are fleeing confusion and the terror of becoming. The loss of friends to addiction becomes another silent sorrow: watching someone disappear while still alive. The body remains; the presence fades. This ambiguous loss fractures trust in relationship itself.

Even more devastating is the loss of friends to suicide—a tragic and increasingly frequent reality among youth. Adolescents overwhelmed by inner conflicts, identity confusion, frustration, or emotional abandonment may come to perceive death as relief from unbearable psychic pain. This is rarely a longing for nonexistence; it is a longing for relief. The red facet of grief here is therefore twofold: mourning the one who died and confronting the terrifying question—*If life was unbearable for them, what about me?*

Suicide introduces the adolescent to raw existential grief. It exposes the fragility of resilience and the danger of confusing despair with identity. Without emotional or existential scaffolding, grief may collapse into nihilism: *If everything ends, why endure?*

At this edge, something paradoxical begins to stir. Not comfort, but interruption. The adolescent senses—often without language—that suffering is not only something to escape, but something that reveals what cannot yet be lived. This is not moral instruction. It is existential pressure. The soul feels summoned to consciousness before it possesses the tools to sustain it. What breaks is not merely hope, but the illusion that pain carries no meaning. In that fracture, awakening begins—not as clarity, but as disturbance.

Within this framework, moral autonomy emerges through discomfort. Suffering exposes unconscious dependencies: on approval, sensation, distraction, or escape. When these collapse, the soul is not being punished; it is being summoned. Grief becomes initiatory.

Across cultures, adolescence has been marked by rites of passage precisely because this is the age of fire. Without initiation, fire consumes. With guidance, fire tempers. Initiation is the moment when suffering begins to educate rather than merely wound. Ancient rites did not romanticize pain; they contained it. Without symbolic containers, awakening becomes chaotic. With guidance, the fire that threatens to destroy becomes the light by which the self first sees itself.

When adolescent grief is silenced, the young person may conclude that their pain is abnormal or shameful. When it is witnessed—by adults capable of tolerating anger without retaliation, listening without minimizing, and naming suffering without moralizing—the fire organizes itself into light. Pain does not define identity; it refines it.

Ultimately, adolescence teaches that identity is not found in flight, disappearance, or conformity to curated images of perfection. It is forged in the difficult act of remaining present while crossing fire. The red facet of grief does not extinguish desire; it educates it. Desire without grounding burns. Desire integrated with meaning illuminates.

What appears as rebellion is often grief searching for language. What appears as excess may be longing without containment. What appears as self-destruction may be the soul's desperate attempt to escape the pain of becoming. In this sense, adolescence does not fully awaken the soul—it shakes it awake from innocence.

The young person begins to sense that life is not merely to be consumed, but confronted. What burns away illusion makes space for discernment. Awakening here is not wisdom; it is the birth of a question: *How shall I live with what I feel?*

Adolescence ends not with certainty, but with the fragile realization that even wounded desire carries the seed of becoming. Yet becoming is not the same as belonging. The fire of adolescence awakens possibility, but it does not yet anchor it. Desire discovers itself, but it has not yet chosen its ground. The storm that once felt like identity must gradually become responsibility.

As red intensity settles into lived consequence, the soul approaches a quieter, more demanding threshold: not *Who am I?* but *What will I build with what I have discovered?*

It is here that the flame of becoming begins to seek commitment, and the next facet of grief reveals itself—not as fire alone, but as a crossing into the light of consequence. The heat of the storm must now become the warmth of the hearth, as red intensity matures into the Orange Facet of adulthood: the crossroads of the heart.

Chapter 4 | The Orange Facet

Adulthood and the Crossroads of the Heart

The prism burns in orange.

Adulthood encounters the grief of responsibility and moral choice.

Here the soul learns consequence.

Adulthood is the crossing where the soul learns that love demands responsibility—and that awakening often begins where comfort ends.

Adulthood does not arrive with the blaze of adolescence. It comes quietly. There is no single threshold that announces it, no mythic gate opening with ceremony. Instead, life accumulates responsibilities until the inner landscape has changed without notice. Days grow heavier with commitments, nights shorter with rest, and the horizon of possibility narrows with each choice. What once felt like infinite becoming begins to feel like consequence.

Sometimes the realization arrives in an ordinary moment. The house is finally quiet after the children have been put to bed. The dishes are washed, the lights dimmed. One sits for a brief instant before sleep, aware that tomorrow will begin again with obligations already waiting. In that silence, without announcement or drama, a subtle recognition arises: life has crossed into another terrain. Adulthood has arrived—not with fanfare, but with the quiet weight of continuity.

The orange facet of grief marks this crossing: the season in which loss is no longer only about what was taken, but also about what was chosen—and what can no longer be chosen again.

Loss in adulthood is complex and layered. It includes the visible losses of people—the death of parents, the illness or passing of partners, the unthinkable loss of a child. But it also includes quieter bereavements that carry no funeral rites: the apparent loss of freedom within marriage or partnership; the loss of ground beneath one's feet when becoming a parent; the contraction of time for friendships, leisure, and spontaneity; the loss of financial stability through job displacement or economic upheaval; the fading of the body's former resilience as health shifts and limits appear. These transitions are not tragedies by definition. They are passages. Every passage exacts a price. Something must be relinquished so that something else may be assumed.

The loss of a life partner is among the most destabilizing experiences of adulthood, not only emotionally but physically. Social and medical research describes what is known as the "widowhood effect": after the death of a spouse, the surviving partner's risk of illness and mortality rises significantly, especially in the first months and years following the loss. This vulnerability is shaped by grief, stress, depression, disrupted routines of care, and the sudden absence of emotional and practical support. The adult loses not only a beloved presence, but a regulating center of daily life. The rupture of shared rhythms—sleep, meals, routines, decision-making—destabilizes the body as well as the soul, revealing how deeply love organizes human existence.

Here, grief takes on a new texture. It is no longer only the ache of absence. It becomes the mourning of former selves. "I lost you" intertwines with "I lost who I was." The adult grieves versions of life that might have been: paths not taken, vocations abandoned, loves that could not be sustained, and identities that no longer fit the demands of reality. This is the grief of consequence—the sorrow that arises not only from fate, but from choice.

From a Jungian perspective, this season is marked by the collapse of the persona. The social mask that once carried the young adult—success, charisma, competence, productivity—begins to crack under the weight of lived complexity. The adult discovers that the roles they perform cannot contain the fullness of the psyche. Loss exposes what the persona concealed: fatigue, resentment, envy, fear, and a quiet longing for meaning. The shadow emerges not as an enemy, but as the neglected interior asking to be seen. When marriage reveals unresolved dependency, when parenthood exposes impatience, or when professional life unveils ethical compromises, the soul encounters its unintegrated aspects. Grief becomes the messenger that the life one is living no longer matches the life the soul is called to inhabit.

Myth speaks eloquently of this moment through the image of the Wounded King, known in the Arthurian Grail legends as the ruler whose unhealed wound renders the land barren. The wound is not merely personal; it symbolizes a fracture between authority and integrity, power and truth. In adulthood, this wounded king lives within the human being who continues to function outwardly while inwardly losing contact with meaning. Careers advance while the heart grows dry; families persist while intimacy thins; social roles endure while the inner landscape becomes desolate. The land of the soul mirrors this misalignment between who one appears to be and who one truly is. Healing does not come through denial of the wound, but through its recognition. The king must acknowledge his injury so that the land may be restored.

The biblical figure of Job offers another powerful mirror of this season of life. Job loses health, security, social status, and companionship. His suffering is not explained; no moral arithmetic accounts for his losses. Adulthood often feels Jobian in this way: one may do "everything right" and still lose what was carefully built. When suffering is stripped of false explanations, it confronts the soul with its deepest dependencies—on control, recognition, stability, and certainty. The spiritual invitation is not to romanticize loss, but to allow it to reorder values. Job's awakening does not occur through answers, but through encounter: a reorientation of consciousness beyond the illusion that life owes comfort.

From a spiritual perspective, adulthood is not merely an accident of time but part of a deeper educational journey. The incarnating soul enters life within particular circumstances—family, body, environment, and challenges—that become the terrain of its development. Loss, in this light, is not evidence of divine indifference but part of the curriculum of maturation. Conflicts often reveal unresolved tendencies and unconscious dependencies. What collapses is not the soul's worth, but the structure that once supported earlier forms of identity.

Adulthood grief often hides behind productivity. Many adults continue to perform while grieving silently. They function; they no longer feel. This emotional numbing is itself a form of loss: the loss of contact with one's inner life. Distraction can become a subtle form of anesthesia—the substitution of busyness, consumption, or compulsive caretaking for genuine inner work. When pain is silenced rather than listened to, it returns in other forms: irritability, depression, somatic symptoms, and relational coldness. Grief that is not integrated becomes character.

The awakening motif speaks directly to this crossroads. The Apostle Paul of Tarsus writes, "Awake, you who sleep, arise from the dead, and Christ will give you light." Beyond its religious context, this call resonates psychologically as a summons to consciousness when life's illusions dissolve. Adulthood is the season when the soul is invited to awaken from the dream that happiness will come from arrangement alone—the right partner, the right career, the right stability.

Joanna de Ângelis, in *Life: Challenges and Solutions*, frames awakening not as mystical escape, but as ethical lucidity: the courage to see oneself without self-deception, to accept responsibility for emotional recovery, and to choose renewal over stagnation. Awakening is the willingness to feel what has long been avoided and to reorganize life around truth rather than habit. Here, grief becomes moral reorientation. The loss of a spouse or child shatters assumptions of permanence; the loss of professional identity confronts the idol of productivity. These losses are not merely events—they are thresholds of ethical maturation. The adult is called to recover agency not by undoing loss, but by choosing how to live with it.

The orange facet of grief carries a sober hope. It does not promise the restoration of what was; it promises the possibility of reorientation. Hope here is not naïve optimism; it is the disciplined choice to awaken. It is the willingness to integrate shadow, to heal the wounded king within, and to endure unanswered questions without surrendering meaning. In this facet, love becomes less impulsive and more intentional. Responsibility replaces illusion.

Loss in adulthood strips life of fantasy but offers something rarer: coherence. When grief is faced, the scattered parts of the self begin to gather around what truly matters. Relationships are chosen with discernment. Work is redefined by service rather than ego. The inner life claims a place alongside outer achievement. The adult begins to recognize that fulfillment is not the absence of pain, but the presence of purpose within it. Life, in this season, is no longer a playground of infinite possibilities; it reveals itself as a school of consciousness. Each responsibility becomes a lesson in love. Each limitation becomes a call to depth.

The orange facet of grief does not promise comfort restored, but meaning reclaimed—the sober hope that, when the ground gives way, the soul can learn to stand by choosing to awaken.

Awakening is not the end of the journey. To stand is not the same as to understand. The labor of adulthood teaches responsibility; it does not automatically grant coherence. After years of striving, building, repairing, and choosing, another movement begins—less visible, less urgent, but more interior. The soul no longer asks only how to endure or how to rebuild, but how to gather what has been lived into meaning. At this point, the next hue of the prism begins to reveal itself — not as effort, but as integration. For what was once the struggle to survive loss slowly transforms into the art of understanding life.

Chapter 5 | The Violet Facet

Maturity and the Season of Integration

The prism softens into violet.

Maturity gathers the grief of time, memory, and unfinished lives.

Here the soul begins to integrate.

Maturity is the season in which the soul ceases to chase what life once promised and begins to harvest what life has patiently taught. If adulthood is the crossroads where responsibility awakens consciousness, maturity is the landscape where consciousness learns to integrate what has been lived. The violet facet of grief corresponds to this threshold of synthesis.

Within the mechanics of the prism, violet light carries the shortest wavelength and the highest frequency; it is the last color visible before the spectrum transitions into the invisible realm. In the architecture of the soul, violet represents this same ethereal boundary:

the threshold where personality becomes less opaque to the deeper light of the Spirit—not fading, but allowing meaning to pass through more freely.

If childhood grief is blue with vulnerability, adolescence red with fire, and adulthood orange with moral crossroads, the season of maturity is violet—the color of twilight, when light softens, contours blur, and meaning deepens. Violet is not the color of disappearance, but of transition. It is the hour when the day does not end abruptly, but slowly releases itself into another form of presence. Born from the union of red and blue, violet embodies the spiritual alchemy of experience: passion tempered by reflection, loss transformed into wisdom, and time transmuted into meaning. It is the hue of spiritual depth, interior authority, and the quiet illumination that emerges when the soul no longer resists what has been.

After the long years of building, striving, sustaining, and enduring, many enter a quieter and less publicly recognized form of grief: the syndrome of the empty nest. Children grow, depart, and begin lives of their own. What remains is not merely the silence of rooms once filled with movement, but an echo within the psyche. Routines that once structured meaning dissolve; identities shaped around care and presence lose their central function. The grief here is not the loss of a person, but the loss of a role—and with it, the loss of a version of oneself.

The question that emerges is subtle yet profound: who am I when the life I built no longer needs me in the same way? This threshold exposes how deeply identity may have been woven into function. The violet facet of grief invites the soul to rediscover itself beyond roles, beyond usefulness as defined by others, and beyond the narrative of indispensability.

This period is often accompanied by physiological and hormonal changes that further unsettle identity. In women, menopause marks not only a biological transition, but a symbolic one: the closing of one cycle of fertility and the opening of another form of generativity—generativity of wisdom, presence, and spiritual creativity. In men, andropause and the gradual shifts in testosterone levels often bring changes in vitality, mood, desire, and self-image. Sexuality itself may change in rhythm, intensity, or expression.

For many, this is experienced as loss: the loss of youthful desire, the loss of bodily responsiveness, the loss of familiar forms of intimacy. Yet here too, the violet facet reframes grief as invitation. These biological shifts are not mere declines, but part of the soul's transcendental itinerary. As urgency wanes, interiority expands. What diminishes in hormonal intensity may deepen in emotional presence, tenderness, and conscious intimacy. The body teaches that eros need not vanish—it transforms. Love becomes less performative and more relational; intimacy shifts from conquest to communion.

In this season, loss no longer arrives as interruption alone; it arrives as accumulation. One does not only grieve a single death or rupture, but the gradual thinning of a world once shared. Friends who once walked beside us begin to depart—some through death, others through illness, others through the quiet distancing that comes with frailty, relocation, or memory's erosion. The mirror no longer reflects the face one once inhabited.

The calendar compresses. Time, which once felt abundant, now feels intimate.

This is not yet the grief of the body's collapse—that belongs to the green facet. The violet facet speaks of something subtler: the grief of witnessing the departure of one's generation, the grief of becoming a survivor of one's own story. These losses of old age are often relational and temporal before they are physical. One begins to lose contemporaries—those who carry shared memories, common references, and familiar laughter. With them disappears not only companionship, but a living archive of one's own past.

This form of grief is rarely dramatic. It is quiet, cumulative, and easily overlooked. There is no single funeral for the loss of "my people." Instead, the world slowly empties of those who once witnessed our lives.

The soul begins to realize that it is becoming the elder in the room—the one who remembers what others no longer lived. This status of survivor carries a quiet and sacred responsibility: to hold the light for the generations coming behind. The elder becomes a bridge for the Blue and Red facets of youth, offering living testimony that storms can be weathered and that meaning survives the fire.

Legacy begins to reveal itself here—not as monument, but as transmission. The mature soul gradually understands that the true measure of a life lies not only in what it accomplished, but in what it leaves alive in others. Values, gestures, acts of courage, quiet examples of integrity—these become seeds carried forward in lives we may never fully witness. In this sense, legacy is not merely memory; it is continuity. Something of the soul's labor remains active in the moral and emotional landscape of the world. The elder begins to perceive that influence does not end with one's presence; it unfolds in the invisible inheritance of character, compassion, and meaning entrusted to those who come after.

And within this thinning of presence, another movement quietly begins. The soul encounters the grief of unrealized lives. Roads not taken, vocations postponed, dreams that dissolved beneath responsibility now return to consciousness. This return can ache. Still, maturity offers a paradoxical gift: the freedom to reinterpret the past without the illusion that it could have been otherwise.

What was not lived becomes material for compassion rather than regret.

The violet facet does not erase longing; it integrates it. The soul learns to honor the lives that were not lived without becoming imprisoned by them.

Philosophical traditions echo this vision of maturity as harvest rather than decline. Marcus Tullius Cicero—the Roman statesman and philosopher—wrote a profound defense of the later years in his work *De Senectute* (On Old Age). Cicero rejected the notion that aging is merely loss, portraying later life as a season of fruition—the harvest of character and ethical refinement cultivated over decades. The fruits of time, he suggested, are not measured by physical vigor but by clarity of judgment, moral discernment, and interior freedom. This vision resonates deeply with the violet facet: the realization that what withers in strength may ripen in insight.

Mythologically, this period corresponds to the archetype of the Wise Elder—the *Senex*. Derived from the Latin term for "old man," the Senex was originally a title of high social standing in Ancient Rome, forming the linguistic root of our modern "Senate." In the landscape of the soul, Carl Jung suggests this archetype appears at the culmination of individuation. It is the moment when the ego no longer competes with the Self, but listens to it.

The Wise Elder emerges when the soul has learned to sit with ambiguity, to hold paradox without fragmentation, and to see suffering not as punishment but as teacher. The elder does not promise comfort; the elder offers coherence.

The myth of Saturn—or Chronos—deepens this symbolic landscape. Saturn devours his children in the ancient myth, embodying the terror of time that consumes all things. Yet Saturn is also the god of agriculture, harvest, and cycles. Time destroys, but time also ripens.

It is here that the orange responsibility of adulthood—the labor of building and sustaining—is transmuted into the violet lucidity of the elder. One no longer works the soil to possess the crop, but to understand the cycle. Chronos is not only the devourer of youth; he is also the teacher of depth.

The violet facet of grief acknowledges this double face of time. What time takes away in immediacy, it offers back in perspective. To mature is to reconcile with Chronos—to cease fighting time and begin learning from it.

Within Spiritist psychology, maturity is not the closing of a life chapter, but the opening of a deeper curriculum of the soul. From this perspective, the incarnating Spirit enters later stages of life with specific educational needs: to loosen attachments to form, to detach identity from roles, to refine emotional bonds, and to cultivate transcendental meaning.

The loss of external demands creates space for inner listening. The soul is gently, and sometimes painfully, redirected from doing toward being.

This redirection often reopens old relational wounds. In maturity, many recognize how much love was lost through pride, silence, or the slow corrosion of unspoken resentments. The violet facet of grief carries within it the ethical invitation of repair. Maturity becomes a season of reevaluation: What truly matters?

The grief of estrangement may now become the doorway to forgiveness. The losses of earlier years invite the recovery of love where love was once neglected—often within the very bosom of family or among friends whose presence was once taken for granted.

Here, grief no longer speaks primarily of what was lost externally, but of what must be integrated internally. The fragmentation of earlier seasons—youth's idealism, adulthood's responsibility, midlife's disillusionment—seeks coherence.

The violet facet is the alchemy of integration. The soul gathers its scattered parts: the child who dreamed, the adult who endured, and the wounded self who survived. None are rejected; all are welcomed into a broader interior wholeness.

The Prism of Grief

Spiritual awakening in maturity often assumes a quieter tone. There are fewer dramatic revelations and more reverent questions. Faith matures into trust; belief matures into lived coherence. Spirituality becomes less about ascent and more about presence.

Loss in this season no longer demands explanation; it invites interpretation. The violet facet does not deny sorrow—it dignifies it as teacher.

The body teaches impermanence.

Relationships teach forgiveness.

Time teaches humility.

Silence teaches depth.

Maturity, as the time of integration, offers the soul a rare gift: reconciliation with its own story. What was broken may not be repaired in form, but it can be healed in meaning.

Old age is the season when the soul begins to learn that holding and letting go are not opposites, but two movements of the same love.

The violet facet does not restore what was; it integrates what has been. In this integration, grief is no longer only the mark of loss—it becomes the signature of wisdom.

Integration, however, is not the final threshold. One may reconcile with memory, forgive the unlived life, and soften into the wisdom of time—and still remain housed in flesh. However translucent the personality becomes in violet light, it is sustained by a body subject to change, decline, and rupture.

Maturity gathers meaning; it does not suspend biology.

As the elder reconciles with Chronos, another confrontation approaches—quieter and more intimate. Not with memory, but with matter. The soul that has integrated its story must now encounter the limits of its vehicle.

The prism turns again—not toward time's harvest, but toward the fragile instrument through which every experience was lived.

If violet refines identity, green tests embodiment.

There comes a moment when the question is no longer, "Who am I beyond my roles?" but, "Who am I when my body no longer obeys my will?"

And so the next facet emerges—not as philosophy, but as flesh.

Chapter 6 | The Green Facet

The Fragile Vessel The Fragile Vessel of the Body

The prism settles into green.

Illness reveals the grief of the body and the limits of incarnation.

Here the soul learns humility.

If the previous facets of the prism have explored the loss of those we love or the roles we inhabit, the Green Facet brings the soul to its most intimate and inescapable frontier: the flesh.

In the spectrum of light, green is the midpoint—the color of the heart's center, the leaf, and the vital energy that sustains life. It represents the "Great Harmony" between spirit and earth—the point where the pulse of the soul meets the rhythm of nature. When this facet becomes clouded by illness, it is not merely a role that is lost; it is the very medium through which we touch, breathe, and exist in the material world.

The grief of health is the mourning of our biological invincibility. It is the moment when the body ceases to be a transparent window and becomes a heavy, opaque wall.

We often mistakenly associate this form of corporeal grief exclusively with the twilight of life. The Green Facet, however, may cast its shadow at any hour. A child born with an impairment, a young adult struck by a chronic condition, or a parent facing the sudden rupture of an accident all inhabit this same landscape.

For most of our lives, the body is a silent servant. We identify ourselves with our strength, our agility, and our capacity to act. The Green Facet begins when this transparency shatters. Suddenly the body demands attention. It speaks through the language of pain, fatigue, and limitation.

The psychological shock of illness is the realization that the will of the Spirit is now constrained by the fragility of the cells. We must grieve the "Self-as-Actor"—the version of ourselves that once moved through the world without hesitation.

Sometimes this realization arrives quietly, in a moment so simple that it almost escapes notice: the first time someone discovers they cannot rise from a chair without help. The hand extended by another becomes both assistance and revelation. What once required no thought now requires humility. In that instant the body ceases to be an obedient instrument and becomes a teacher. The soul confronts a new truth: independence was never as absolute as we imagined.

This loss requires a profound psychological reorganization. We must learn to be "someone" even when we can no longer "do" anything.

This struggle deepens when the instrument of the body fails not only in movement but in cognition. When memory begins to erode, when the threads of recognition fray, and when the mind becomes a labyrinth, a double grief emerges. The individual suffers the slow dismantling of their history, while the family enters what psychologists call ambiguous loss—mourning someone who is still physically present.

For the family, the person they once knew is gradually replaced by a stranger inhabiting a familiar form. The caregiver must navigate a strange and exhausting landscape where devotion must be offered to a presence that can no longer return recognition. This may be the ultimate test of ethical love: to care for the Spirit even when the mask of personality has become unrecognizable.

The weight of this transition often falls upon the family, creating a collective grief that is rarely named. There is a quiet guilt that accompanies the exhaustion of caregiving—a mourning of one's own freedom, time, and peace.

A deeper spiritual perspective invites us to see this not as a tragic accident, but as part of a shared human curriculum. The illness of one member becomes a laboratory for the spiritual progress of the entire group. It forces a confrontation with the illusion of independence. We learn that we are, in truth, radically dependent on one another.

The family becomes a living ecosystem of patience, where the "healthy" learn the sanctity of service and the "ill" learn the difficult humility of being served.

It is often within this climate of exhaustion, fear, and helplessness that the question of euthanasia may surface—whether as a personal temptation for the one who suffers or as a silent consideration within the family circle. Even in fragility, life remains meaningful.

The waters of physical or mental decay are difficult to navigate, but they are still waters of learning. The lessons of this phase are slower, humbler, more interior—no less essential within the itinerary of the soul.

From a Spiritist ethical perspective, we are invited not to contemplate euthanasia or cultivate the desire for death, but to reverence the body as a sacred instrument of experience and repair. Respecting the body does not mean idolizing biological survival at any cost; refusing euthanasia is not the same as demanding the prolongation of artificial life through disproportionate or invasive means.

There is a moral difference between allowing natural death to unfold with compassion and prematurely interrupting the course of life.

Beyond the immediate ethical dimension, euthanasia also leaves a pedagogical echo within the moral fabric of the family and community. The soul does not merely depart from an experience—it departs carrying the imprint of how that experience was concluded.

Drawn deeper into this chapter of the flesh, the soul encounters another poignant shadow: the shrinking of the relational world. Illness often transforms the social landscape into a desert. Friends visit less frequently. Conversations shorten. The room grows quieter.

The sickroom becomes a kind of monastery—though one the soul never chose to enter.

Yet even this isolation holds meaning within the architecture of the prism. When the world no longer comes toward us, we are invited to travel inward.

To understand the meaning of this physical rupture, we may turn to the ancient archetype of Chiron.

In Greek mythology, Chiron was a centaur—half divine, half animal—who was accidentally struck by a poisoned arrow. Because he was immortal, he could not die; because the poison was incurable, he was condemned to live at the intersection of divinity and agony.

Chiron did not spend his life seeking a cure for his wound.

Instead, he sought understanding.

He withdrew into a cave and transformed suffering into a laboratory of wisdom.

In this sense, Chiron reveals something essential about the Green Facet: the wound that cannot be healed may still become the place from which healing radiates. What the body cannot repair, the soul can transform into vision. The wounded one becomes capable of guiding others not despite the wound, but through it.

In the Green Facet, illness becomes our poisoned arrow. It is the moment we realize that some things in life cannot be fixed—only carried.

The wound may open a second sight: the capacity to perceive the essential because the superficial has been stripped away.

The sickroom, the wheelchair, the quiet endurance of limitation may become caves of prophecy where the soul learns that the wound is not merely a mistake, but a portal.

The body is an instrument, not the musician.

When the instrument falters, the music must change.

Illness becomes an invitation to inner reorganization. As the body weakens, the Spirit withdraws energy from the periphery and concentrates it at the center.

This is the paradox of the Green Facet: while the flesh weakens, the essential consciousness may deepen in lucidity.

The body reveals itself as a temporary envelope—designed to carry us through the terrain of material life. Its gradual decline may not be simple deterioration, but the ripening of the immortal traveler.

We are slowly being unpacked from the physical world.

The knots of matter loosen.

The transition becomes less rupture and more return.

For those watching a loved one lose memory, there is comfort in remembering that the Spirit forgets nothing. Every act of love, every whispered prayer, every moment of patient care is woven into the deeper fabric of being.

The Green Facet does not ask us to celebrate suffering. But it invites us to honor the transformation it demands.

It teaches the grace of dependency.

For the one who spent a lifetime being the pillar, the loss of health becomes the school where they learn the sacred art of receiving love without earning it through work.

We discover the body as a guest—one to be treated with tenderness even as it falters.

Vitality is no longer measured by strength. It is measured by the capacity to forgive, to hope, and to remain inwardly at peace.

Ultimately the Green Facet reveals that the driver is more than the vehicle.

When the car can no longer move, the driver prepares to step outside.

And look at the stars.

To lose health or memory is to begin the final movement of the prism—where the light no longer needs glass to show its colors.

It begins to shine on its own.

Illness confronts us with the limits of the body. There are also seasons when the body remains capable, the mind lucid, the hands steady—while something else begins to dissolve.

The crisis is no longer biological.

It is existential.

One is still alive, still thinking, still able—and yet no longer central.

The question shifts—not, "Can I still move?"

But:

"Am I still needed?"

Here the prism turns again. Green reveals the fragility of the vehicle. Another loss waits quietly beyond illness: the loss of function, relevance, and social usefulness.

If Green humbles the body, Yellow will challenge the identity that once depended on being necessary.

And in that turning, the soul must face another silence.

Chapter 7 | The Yellow Facet

The Loss of Work, Role, and Status

The prism brightens into yellow.

Later life confronts the grief of usefulness and social centrality.

Here the soul asks a new question: Who am I when I am no longer needed?

In the spectrum of the prism, yellow is the color of the sun at its zenith—it represents the light of our midday, the period of life when we shine most brightly in the eyes of society. This is the facet of our doing. It encompasses the careers we built, the titles we carried, the authority we wielded, and the social status that often served as our armor.

When this facet becomes clouded by loss—whether through retirement, unemployment, or the natural stepping back that comes with age—the soul faces a crisis of usefulness. The central, haunting question of the Yellow Facet becomes: "Who am I if I am no longer productive?"

For many, this is the most terrifying silence of all, because in a world that equates value with output, the cessation of work can feel like the cessation of existence itself.

For the modern ego, this loss is often experienced as a catastrophic collapse. Carl Jung spoke profoundly of "ego inflation," a state in which we become so identified with our social role—the Persona—that we forget there is a human being beneath the armor. We do not merely have a job; we become the job. We do not merely hold authority; we begin to measure our very worth by the power we command.

This is the "solar trap" of the Yellow Facet: the higher we rise in the eyes of the world, the further we have to fall when the stage is inevitably dismantled.

When the office door closes for the last time, or when a younger generation steps into the space we once occupied, the sensation can be one of sudden, cold withdrawal. As the curtain falls on our professional act, we see new faces take their place under the spotlight, speaking the lines we once spoke and making the decisions we once made. In this moment, a chilling sense of oblivion can set in—the fear that we have been erased, that our name has been struck from the ledger of the living world. We become spectators at a play we once directed, relegated to the shadows of the wings while the performance carries on without us.

Yet the "curtain call" of our professional life is not the end of the Spirit's agency. Retiring or stepping back does not mean the loss of one's faculties; our intelligence, our hard-won competence, the dexterity of our hands, and the vast library of our experience remain intact. They have simply been liberated from the constraints of the marketplace. The "oblivion" we fear is merely the ego's reaction to the loss of a title—it is not a reflection of the Spirit's capacity.

This transition is captured with devastating clarity in William Shakespeare's tragedy *King Lear*. Lear is a man who believes he is his crown, confusing the respect paid to his office with the love due to his soul. When he surrenders his power and is stripped of his knights, his land, and his status, he descends into a literal and metaphorical storm of madness. Yet it is only in this fall from the false throne that Lear begins to develop a heart.

In the wreckage of his status, wandering the heath as a "poor, bare, forked animal," he finally discovers his humanity. The Yellow Facet teaches us that the storm of losing our professional identity is often the only environment in which the soul can learn that dignity does not depend on a title, but on the capacity to remain present.

In truth, the closing of one door is the opening of a new world—one that may not offer high salaries or impressive titles, but where we can finally make a profound, soul-level difference. This is the realm of the true calling.

In the midday of life, we often spend decades misplaced, searching for validation in sources that do not nourish our true inclinations. We chase what the marketplace values rather than what our Spirit requires. The loss of status is frequently the universe's way of correcting our path. It is the moment when the external noise of "should" is silenced so that the inner call of "must" can finally be heard.

History is replete with those who were deemed failures by the narrow standards of their time, only to reveal a light that changed the world. We remember Albert Einstein, who struggled within the rigid walls of traditional schooling. Had he succeeded in becoming the model student society demanded, he might have spent his life as a quiet academic rather than the visionary who reshaped our understanding of the universe. His "failure" to fit the mold allowed him to preserve the genius that belonged to his inner call.

When we lose our place in the societal hierarchy, we are not losing our ability to contribute; we are being redirected toward a contribution that only we can make.

A spiritually grounded ethical perspective offers a vital corrective to this grief. We are reminded that we never truly lose what we have learned. Every struggle with a difficult manager, every late night spent mastering a craft, becomes an interior acquisition—woven not into a résumé, but into character. This wealth is not tied to the paycheck; it becomes part of who we are. The loss of a social role can thus be understood not as diminishment, but as an invitation—a shift from having to being.

Perhaps the greatest illusion of modern culture is the belief that a person's value depends on what they produce. Yet the qualities most essential to human life — patience, listening, wisdom, compassion — rarely appear in productivity reports. They flourish in the quiet of relationships and mature precisely when the urgency of performance no longer dominates our days.

This is an invitation to become more than a producer; it is an invitation to become a participant in the life of society. The world is hungry for the very talents the marketplace no longer buys. In NGOs, in community centers, and in the lives of the youth, experience becomes a lighthouse. When we offer our hands to help a child or our wisdom to steady a community, we are no longer working for a boss—we are working for the Spirit of Humanity.

In these spaces, talents are not merely used; they are appreciated for their intrinsic worth. We discover that our value was never in the "impact" of our title, but in the impact of our kindness and commitment.

The dignity of the individual is intrinsic; it is a spark of the Divine that remains undimmed whether one sits on a throne or in a quiet room. We discover that we can be a "genius" in the art of living simply because we have finally aligned with our true nature.

This alignment is the gold that remains after the yellow sun of the midday world has set. We learn that work was merely a temporary stage, a vessel for growth, but never the passenger itself. The most important work of our life was never the one listed on our résumé; it was the work of becoming a Spirit capable of existing in the light, even when the world's applause has faded into silence.

Ultimately, the loss of status is a process of right-sizing the ego. When the curtain falls on our professional life, we take off the heavy costume of the "Producer" and step out into the cool evening air of our true identity. We discover that we are still here—whole, worthy, and deeply loved—not for what we do, but for the simple, magnificent fact that we are.

The Yellow Facet reveals that the true measure of a life is not how much we produced for the world, but how much we allowed the world to produce a deeper, more authentic, and more serviceable Spirit within us.

The loss of work is not the final dismantling of the persona. One may step away from titles, surrender authority, and survive the quieting of applause—yet still remain bound to another surface: the image one presents to the world.

If Yellow confronts us with the question, "Who am I when I no longer produce?" another question soon follows, more intimate and less publicly spoken: "Who am I when I no longer dazzle?"

There are seasons when one is no longer central in function, yet still invested in reflection. The role may fall away, but the mirror remains; and as long as we seek confirmation in the gaze of others, the ego quietly finds new ground upon which to rebuild its identity.

The prism turns again—not toward usefulness, but toward visibility.

For beyond the loss of status lies a quieter grief: the fading of youth, the erosion of beauty, and the slow withdrawal of desirability. If Yellow dims the sun of productivity, Silver clouds the mirror of appearance. And in that clouding, the soul must confront not what it does, but how it believes it is seen.

Chapter 8 | The Silver Facet

The Mirror of Narcissus and the Gift of Time

The prism gleams in silver.

Aging reveals the grief of the reflected self and the fading of outward beauty.

Here the soul learns to move from being seen to being known.

If the previous facets of the prism have explored the weight of death and the frailty of health, the Silver Facet turns toward a quieter disappearance: the vanishing of youth, the erosion of beauty, and the slow withdrawal of desirability. This is the grief of the "Reflected Self."

In the anatomy of grief, there is a loss that is rarely mourned in public, yet it haunts the private corridors of the mind—the loss of one's own reflection. It is the moment we realize that the face looking back at us from the glass is no longer the face we feel we inhabit. The mirror begins to tell a story that the inner self has not yet learned to accept. Within the prism, this facet marks the transition from external shimmer to inner light.

We call this the Silver Facet because silver is the material that gives a mirror its power; it is the opaque backing that allows the glass to reflect the world. In the autumn of life, this silver appears in our own crowning glory—the strands of silver hair that begin to frame the face. We often treat these threads as signs of depletion, yet they are, in truth, the silvering of the soul's mirror.

Just as the silver backing of a mirror must be removed if one is ever to see through the glass into deeper reality, we too must move beyond our obsession with the surface to perceive the spirit beneath.

To understand the nature of this attachment, we must revisit the myth of Narcissus. We often misinterpret Narcissism as mere vanity, but the myth tells a far more tragic story of disconnection. Narcissus did not love himself; he loved an image that he did not realize was his own. He was captivated by a surface—a reflection in a pool of water that was fragile, two-dimensional, and entirely dependent on the stillness of the water. Narcissus died not because he was in love, but because he was trapped. He could not touch the image he loved, and he could not look away from it to discover the living, breathing being who stood on the bank.

If Narcissus represents the distraction of the image, a much darker warning appears in Oscar Wilde's masterpiece, *The Picture of Dorian Gray*. In this narrative, a handsome young man makes a fateful wish: that he might remain forever young while his painted portrait bears the burden of his aging and his sins. Dorian succeeds in "freezing" his Silver Facet; his physical reflection remains flawless and radiant for decades.

However, this victory becomes a spiritual catastrophe. Because he refuses to allow his body to reflect his history, his soul becomes a monster. Wilde shows us that the attempt to stop the clock is an act of violence against the soul. When we refuse to age, we refuse to evolve. Aging is the mechanism that keeps us honest; it ensures that our outer life eventually aligns with our inner reality.

In an era of digital filters and surgical "corrections," the Silver Facet reminds us that a face without a history is a soul without a map. To erase the wrinkle is to silence the story. The Silver Facet is the crisis that occurs when the "pool" begins to ripple and the portrait begins to change.

It begins quietly, often with the first wrinkles—those uninvited guests that map out a history we are not always ready to read. We experience these marks of time as a betrayal, a sudden leak in the vessel of youth. Yet these marks are a sacred cartography of the life that has been lived. A wrinkle is the physical residue of a thousand smiles, a myriad of worries, and the weight of countless gazes. It is the skin's way of losing elasticity so that the Spirit may gain depth.

When the hair turns to silver, it is as if the body is finally putting on its royal robes of experience. If our identity is rooted entirely in the smooth, unwritten surface of the past, the arrival of these silver threads can feel like the dissolution of the self. This creates a profound psychological conflict, for in a society that worships the "cult of youth," beauty functions as a form of currency. When beauty fades, many experience a kind of social invisibility, leading to the terrifying question: If I am no longer beautiful to the world, am I still valuable to myself?

In reality, the "loss" of form is rarely a simple subtraction; it is often a sacred exchange. Perhaps the most profound example appears in the image of a pregnant woman. As her body expands, the "idealized" form she once possessed is temporarily surrendered. Yet this apparent loss melts the heart of the observer. We look at her with awe because we see that her body is being offered to bring new life into the world. Her loss becomes another's beginning. This is the ultimate parable of the flesh: the body is designed to be spent in the service of love.

There is a contemporary story that captures the healing of this facet more vividly than any ancient myth. A young girl accidentally knocked a beautiful mirror off the wall. As it shattered, she began to cry. Her grandmother found her there, knelt down, and said softly: "Do not cry, my dear. The mirror is in pieces, but look at you—you are still whole here. You are not the pieces on the floor."

This realization—that we are the observer, not the reflection—is the first step toward freedom. But the second step is even more profound, and it is beautifully illustrated in the ancient Japanese art of Kintsugi.

In Kintsugi, when a ceramic bowl breaks, the craftsman does not attempt to hide the cracks. Instead, the fractures are repaired with lacquer mixed with powdered gold. The philosophy is that the piece becomes more beautiful for having been broken. The gold does not restore the bowl to its original state; it transforms it into something far more precious.

In the Silver Facet, our lives resemble Kintsugi. Our wrinkles, our silver hair, and the scars of our experiences are the cracks in our vessel. Spiritist psychology invites us to fill those fractures with the gold of wisdom, compassion, and resilience.

Facing these changes is undeniably difficult—a series of quiet, daily farewells to the versions of ourselves we once knew. Yet within this passage there is also a hidden liberation. Spiritual reflection and psychological insight remind us that the physical body is not the totality of our being, but a temporary and purposeful garment. Beneath this changing surface resides the Spirit—the enduring self that is not diminished by time and remains untouched by the biological laws of decay.

In this light, aging is not a process of depletion, but one of refinement. As the mask grows more fragile and transparent, it begins to reveal a beauty that youth cannot possess—a spiritual aesthetic born of experience.

Ultimately, the Silver Facet teaches us to move from wanting to be seen to wanting to be known. We realize that the body is not the Self, but the Temple.

Consider the mystery of sea glass. It begins its life as something industrial and sharp. It enters the ocean as a broken thing, jagged and dangerous. But through decades of relentless tumbling in the rough surf, the waves do not destroy the glass; they refine it. The sharp edges are ground away by the sand, leaving behind a distinctive frosted surface. What was once clear and reflective becomes opaque and soft; what was once dangerous becomes a gem.

We, too, are like sea glass. We lose our "perfection"—our sharp youthful edges and our clear, vanity-driven reflections—to the tumbling of life's difficult years. Yet in that process we gain our true value. We become gems that no longer obsess over surface reflection because we have become vessels for the light that passes through.

When the mirror finally breaks, we do not disappear into oblivion. We simply stop staring at the fragments on the floor and begin to see the life that remains—weathered by the waves, filled with the gold of Kintsugi, and standing whole, radiant, and eternal in the center of the room.

Yet there is a danger hidden even within the refinement of silver.

To release attachment to youth is liberating. To accept the changing mirror is maturation. But if identity was too long anchored in what was lost—whether beauty, role, vitality, or recognition—the withdrawal of those reflections may leave behind more than humility; it may leave vacancy.

There are moments when the mirror does not merely dim but ceases to return n image at all. One no longer grieves a wrinkle or a fading role; one begins to grieve the disappearance of the self that once animated them. The prism darkens not because light has vanished from the world, but because it is no longer being reflected.

When grief ceases to move, when mourning ceases to breathe, when sorrow becomes structure rather than passage, the soul enters another terrain—not the twilight of maturity nor the silvering of wisdom, but the absorption of light.

And thus emerges the next refraction: the Dark Facet.

Chapter 9 | The Dark Facet

Complicated Grief and Depression

The prism darkens into shadow.

Grief becomes heavy enough to absorb the light of meaning.

Here the soul confronts the danger of losing itself.

In the spectrum of the prism, the Dark Facet represents the absorption of light. In classical physics, black is not truly a color but a condition in which incoming light is taken in and nothing is reflected back. It is a state of total consumption.

In the itinerary of the soul, this corresponds to the realm of complicated grief and deep depression—the "Grey Cloud" that descends when mourning ceases to be a journey and becomes a permanent residence. This is a terrifying loss because it is not merely the loss of someone or something; it is the loss of the self that once knew how to live with that absence.

We do not only lose a loved one, a role, or a sense of stability. We lose the vantage point from which we once experienced the world. The "I" that once navigated life begins to dissolve into shadow, until we become almost indistinguishable from the darkness we inhabit. In this state, the soul approaches a kind of spiritual absolute zero—a condition where the movement of hope slows to a halt and the heart enters a profound interior winter.

When we are caught in this facet, pain can become our only reliable identity. We settle into what might be called victim consciousness, surrendering our inner agency to the tragedy that befell us. We move through the world like ghosts—physically present, yet emotionally frozen.

This condition is captured in the ancient Greek tragedy of Niobe. A queen who lost all her children to divine wrath, Niobe did not simply mourn; she was consumed by her sorrow until even her biology yielded to despair. The myth tells us that she fled to Mount Sipylus and was transformed into stone. She became the "Weeping Rock," a monument of unyielding sorrow that continued to shed tears even as it stood lifeless.

Niobe represents the archetype of the soul that has calcified in order to protect itself from further feeling, yet continues to bleed internally. To the person inhabiting the Dark Facet, the stone becomes a defense: *If I am stone, I cannot be hurt again. If I am stone, I no longer have to endure the changing seasons of a world that dared to continue turning after mine had stopped.*

In this state, the individual often loses the future tense of their own vocabulary. The mind becomes a closed loop, endlessly orbiting the moment of impact. The tragedy is no longer something that happened in the past; it becomes a permanent *now*. Time itself appears arrested.

This psychic stasis creates another subtle trap: the belief that healing would be an act of betrayal. If the pain softens, the person fears the memory of what was lost might fade as well. Thus the darkness is guarded as though it were a sacred relic. This is what might be called the "narcissism of agony." Our suffering becomes so vast, so singular, that it seems to eclipse the suffering of all others. We begin to believe our pain grants us a kind of tragic exemption from the responsibilities of living or loving again.

Spiritist psychology suggests that such stagnation often reflects a form of existential rebellion. It is a silent refusal to accept the laws of transition that govern existence. A cycle has ended, yet we refuse to acknowledge its closure. In that refusal, we construct a psychic dam against the flow of life.

Grief then becomes a shield—something that protects us from the terrifying responsibility of beginning again. In some cases, sorrow becomes strangely familiar, even addictive, because it is the only state that feels authentic in a world that has become unrecognizable.

Within this frequency of mind, we may also enter a condition of mental and spiritual parasitism. Sustained in a low vibrational pattern of thought and emotion, the mind becomes increasingly synchronized with similar frequencies from both the internal subconscious and the surrounding environment. Instead of lifting the spirit, these patterns gradually reinforce the heaviness of the inner atmosphere.

The Dark Facet also manifests as a shutdown of the senses. The Grey Cloud acts like a filter that drains color from the world. Food loses its flavor. Music becomes noise. The beauty of nature feels strangely irrelevant, sometimes even offensive to the internal gloom.

This is the petrification of the senses, when the soul retreats so deeply into its interior that the external world can no longer nourish it. The individual is not simply sad; they feel displaced from life itself.

Yet even here, transformation remains possible.

It is important to say clearly that despair itself is not inherently good. The Dark Facet is painful, exhausting, and often terrifying. But within the great book of nature we find a revealing pattern: some of the most profound transformations occur in darkness.

A seed does not germinate in sunlight; it breaks open beneath the soil. The caterpillar does not grow wings in daylight; it dissolves entirely within the darkness of the chrysalis.

The same may be true of the human spirit. What appears to be an absolute night of the soul is not always a state of death. It may instead be a state of incubation. Beneath the stillness of despair, unseen restructuring can take place—a slow reorganization of the foundations of the self.

Modern psychology recognizes a similar phenomenon known as post-traumatic growth. Research suggests that individuals who navigate profound loss sometimes emerge with a deeper resilience, greater compassion, and a renewed sense of purpose. As Martin Luther King Jr. once observed, *"Only when it is dark enough can you see the stars."*

Breaking free from the Dark Facet, however, rarely occurs through passive waiting alone. Because the soul has become immobilized, healing often requires a threefold awakening: psychological support, spiritual re-education, and ethical action.

Professional therapy can help disentangle the identity that has become fused with the trauma. The loss itself may be real and devastating, but the identity constructed around that loss can become a prison. Therapy is the slow and careful work of chipping away at the stone of Niobe until living tissue can breathe again.

Spiritual re-education restores perspective. It reminds the immortal spirit that no loss is final and that the Grey Cloud is only a temporary weather pattern, not the sky itself. If we accept the continuity of the soul, we must also recognize that our stagnation serves neither ourselves nor those we have lost. If our loved ones continue in light, our refusal to live cannot honor them.

Finally, healing requires movement toward ethical engagement with life. The heart that has petrified often softens when it is used in the service of others. The act of alleviating another person's burden disrupts the closed loop of self-absorption that feeds despair.

This is the Law of Labor in its most luminous expression: the work of the soul returning to the living current of existence.

The Dark Facet, therefore, is not a black hole. It can become fertile soil.

You are not being buried; you are being planted.

The Weeping Rock of Niobe is not your final destination. Beneath the stone, the heartbeat of the spirit continues, gathering strength to break through the crust of despair. The darkness does not exist so that you may return to the person you once were; it exists so that you may emerge as someone capable of reaching toward a larger sun.

When the Dark Facet begins to loosen its grip—when the stone softens and the buried seed begins to stir—another question inevitably arises.

It is no longer simply, *"How do I survive this loss?"*

A deeper question emerges:

"What was the nature of the bond that made this loss so devastating?"

For beneath the collapse of identity and the petrification of hope lies something more elemental than grief itself: attachment.

We do not descend into darkness solely because something ended. We descend because something within us was intertwined with what ended.

The prism, having absorbed the light, now turns inward—not toward pathology, but toward structure.

What binds human beings to one another?

What makes love luminous in one season and suffocating in another?

Why does the thread that once sustained us begin to feel like a tether when separation arrives?

To understand the shadow, we must examine the thread.

And thus the prism turns again, revealing the next facet—not the darkness of despair, but the architecture of connection.

Chapter 10 | The Thread

Attachment, Love, and Fear of Separation

The prism reveals a thread of light.

Love binds souls across time, yet fear tightens the knot.

Here the heart must learn the difference between connection and possession.

In the architecture of the prism, if the previous facets have dealt with the external impacts of loss—the fracturing of health, the vanishing of professional status, or the fading of physical vitality—this facet turns the gaze inward to the nature of the bond itself. Every relationship, whether with a person, a career, or a cherished version of ourselves, is held together by an invisible thread of energy—a psychic and spiritual resonance that defies the physical boundaries of skin and bone.

In its healthiest state, this thread is flexible and luminous. It is a golden mean that allows for distance, personal growth, and the rhythmic movement of two distinct beings. It functions much like the string of a musical instrument: it requires a certain amount of tension to produce a note, but it must never be pulled so tight that it snaps, nor so loose that it falls silent.

Yet when grief is anticipated or experienced through the lens of fear, that thread undergoes a dangerous transformation. It ceases to be a connection and becomes a tether. The core question of this facet is one that haunts the human heart:

Why does love—and the loss of what we love—hurt so deeply when it clings?

To answer this, we must distinguish between the Love that Liberates and the Attachment that Imprisons. Love is expansive and solar. It seeks the well-being and evolution of the other, even if that evolution leads them along a different path or into another state of existence. Attachment, by contrast, is a contract of the ego rooted in the fear of the void. We do not cling because we love more intensely; we cling because we fear who we might become without the other. People, roles, or identities quietly become scaffolding for our sense of worth.

Much of the suffering surrounding loss originates in an unspoken Contract of Permanence that we sign with the world. This silent contract demands: *You must never change. You must never leave.* Yet this is a demand for the impossible—a defiance of the fundamental law of movement that governs the universe. Suffering arises from the friction between our longing for permanence and reality's continuous transformation.

Healing requires replacing this contract with something more humble and more sacred: a Covenant of Presence. A covenant does not promise duration or guarantee an outcome. Instead, it is a conscious agreement to be fully present in the living moment of connection, knowing that all forms are temporary.

Psychologically, the refusal to move from contract to covenant leads to Emotional Fusion, a state in which the boundaries between the "I" and the "Thou" collapse into a chaotic singularity. We begin to believe that our happiness, our stability, and even our identity depend entirely upon the presence of the other. When that person leaves—or when health fails or a career ends—the experience is not merely sadness. It feels like an amputation.

We have previously touched upon the "phantom limb" of grief. Here we encounter its energetic root: the mind continues sending signals of expectation into a space where no receiver remains. This is the clinging that produces the most agonizing forms of grief. We are not merely mourning a person or a role—we are mourning what we mistakenly treated as a vital organ of our own psyche.

Mature love understands something different. It recognizes that two complete beings have chosen to walk together. The form of the relationship may change, yet the value and essence of the spirit remain intact.

To move toward liberation, we must identify and untie what might be called the Three Knots of Attachment—a synthesis inspired by Murray Bowen's research on emotional fusion, the psychological reflections on individuation within Spiritist thought, and the mythic curriculum of the soul explored by Robert

A. Johnson in his interpretation of the myth of Eros and Psyche.

These knots represent the places where the energy of our lives becomes entangled in the past.

The first is the Knot of Guilt—the persistent thought: *"I should have done more."*

This knot binds the mind to a past we cannot change. It often rests on the subtle illusion that we controlled another person's destiny or the trajectory of our own health. Accepting that we did not possess such power is not defeat; it is humility before the cycles of life.

The second knot is the Knot of Identity—the haunting question: *"Who am I without them?"*

Here our sense of self becomes dependent on another person or a particular role. If our identity collapses when the other disappears, then that identity was never fully ours—it was a mask worn in relation to them. Untying this knot requires the courageous work of individuation, reclaiming the parts of ourselves we projected onto people, positions, or expectations. The other was never the source of our light; they were the mirror that allowed us to see it. When the mirror moves, the light remains with its source.

The third knot is the Knot of Unfinished Words—the feeling that something essential was left unsaid. This knot builds an illusory wall of silence. We remain tethered to the moment because we imagine communication ended with physical absence. Yet the deepest forms of communication often transcend language itself. We cling to the unsaid because it allows us to postpone saying goodbye.

The myth of Eros and Psyche offers a powerful symbolic map for this entire struggle. Psyche, a mortal woman, becomes the secret bride of Eros, the god of Love, under one condition: she must never look upon his face. Driven by the same fear of uncertainty that fuels possessive attachment, Psyche eventually lights a lamp while Eros sleeps. A drop of hot oil falls onto his shoulder, and wounded by her lack of trust, he flies away.

Psyche's long journey to win him back becomes the soul's curriculum in love matured through suffering. She must complete impossible tasks: sorting seeds of desire, gathering golden wool without being consumed by power, containing the flow of overwhelming emotion, and descending into the underworld to confront death itself. The myth reveals a profound truth: love cannot survive where trust is replaced by control. When we attempt to illuminate every mystery of life with the lamp of certainty, we often burn the very thing we wished to preserve.

From a Spiritist perspective, this psychological evolution toward detachment reflects a broader law of the soul's development. Human beings come together not to possess one another, but to learn how to love as autonomous spirits. Possession, in this sense, becomes the grave of love. When we treat a person, a talent, or a role as something we own, we violate the fundamental liberty that governs the spiritual universe.

The grief that follows the breaking of possessive bonds is painful, yet that rupture can also become the beginning of freedom. For the essential thread of love is never truly severed. When a bond is built on affinity rather than need, it survives the physical veil of death. Only the knots of possession break.

When we release the desire to control what we have lost, we often discover that its essence becomes more present than ever before. We move from the struggle of having toward the quiet peace of communion.

This insight is beautifully echoed in the myth of Ariadne's thread. Ariadne gave Theseus a thread not to trap him inside the Labyrinth, but to guide him safely through it. Our relationships—whether with people, roles, or even our bodies—are meant to function in the same way. They are guides through experience, not the destination itself.

Yet grief often leaves us wandering the maze because we cling to the thread as though it were the path itself. We grip it so tightly that we stop moving forward.

Healing requires a different gesture: we must learn not merely to hold the thread, but to weave it. Memories, losses, and loves become threads in the tapestry of our becoming. Objects, roles, and identities carry only the value we assign to them. With time, we must release certain patterns in order to weave new meaning.

Letting go, then, is not destruction. It is transformation.

Awakening through the Thread means recognizing that no human being, no profession, and no physical condition can be the ultimate source of our light. They are mirrors reflecting a radiance we already carry. Like Psyche, we must complete the tasks of grief until we meet love not as a master or a crutch, but as an equal.

When we finally loosen our closed fist, the thread does not disappear. It rests lightly in the open palm.

It becomes a bridge of light between two travelers—forever connected, yet forever free.

Even when attachment matures into presence, however, another threshold remains.

There comes a moment when the fear of separation is no longer hypothetical. The question shifts from *"What if I lose you?"* to something far more immediate:

What becomes of love when the beloved is no longer physically here?

The thread stretches toward a horizon it cannot fully cross.

At that horizon, the soul encounters a quiet interval—an empty space where the thread seems to dissolve and where meaning is no longer sustained by presence alone.

It is there that another dimension of grief emerges: not only the pain of what has been lost, but the silence of what never came to be.

Before the soul can approach the deeper mystery beyond separation, it must first learn to stand within that interval—the space we may call the Void.

Chapter 11 | The Void

The Grief of What Never Was

The Void is the absence of light.

Not darkness, for darkness still reflects color, but a transparent emptiness. Within the architecture of the prism it is not a color at all. It is the silent interval between colors, the place where light does not arrive.

In this sense, the Void reminds us that some forms of grief are not events, but silences.

Not all grief arises from something that once existed. Some forms of sorrow emerge from what never came to be.

Within the landscape of human experience, there are absences that leave no visible trace. No death has occurred. No object has been broken. No farewell has been spoken. And yet the heart may still feel a quiet and persistent loss.

The child who was never born.

The love that never arrived.

The vocation that remained only a dream.

The sibling who never shared our childhood.

The life we imagined but never inhabited.

These losses are often difficult to name because they have no clear event to mark them. There is no funeral for the life we did not live, no photograph of the child who never existed, no anniversary for the path that quietly disappeared. The world tends to recognize grief when something visible is lost, but it struggles to acknowledge sorrow for possibilities that never took form.

The human soul does not live only in what has happened. It also lives in what it hoped might happen.

Every life contains silent architectures of expectation. From an early age we begin constructing inner landscapes of the future: relationships we believe we will form, work we imagine ourselves doing, families we assume will grow around us, places where we expect to belong. These imagined futures are rarely idle fantasies. They become part of our identity. We grow toward them, orient our choices around them, and quietly weave them into the meaning of our lives.

When such possibilities never materialize, the absence they leave behind can be deeply felt.

A person may carry the quiet grief of a vocation never realized—the artist who never found the courage or opportunity to create, the doctor who never entered the profession that once called to them, the teacher who imagined a life guiding others but was led instead down a different road.

Another may experience the sorrow of migration and the loss of homeland. The departure may have been necessary, even hopeful. Still, something remains suspended in memory: the language spoken without effort, the familiar streets of childhood, the sense of belonging that once existed without question. Life continues elsewhere, but part of the imagined future tied to that place quietly dissolves.

Others carry the weight of paths abandoned for responsibility. A dream set aside in order to care for parents, to provide stability for children, or simply to answer the demands of circumstance. The sacrifice may have been freely chosen and even noble, yet somewhere within the soul another life still lingers, like a story whose final chapter was never written.

The Void is the grief of unlived life.

Because it has no concrete form, this grief often remains invisible both to others and to ourselves. We may not even recognize it as grief. Instead it appears as a subtle restlessness, a quiet comparison between the life that is and the life that might have been.

Modern psychology has attempted to give language to experiences like this. Researchers sometimes speak of *disenfranchised grief*, referring to losses that society does not openly acknowledge or support. When sorrow does not correspond to a recognizable event, it may remain unspoken, leaving the person who experiences it without the communal rituals that normally help grief find expression.

The Prism of Grief

Closely related is the idea of *ambiguous grief*, a form of sorrow that lacks clear boundaries or a tangible object. In such cases the loss is not easily defined. What is mourned may be a possibility, a relationship, or a life trajectory that never fully emerged.

These concepts illuminate something important about the human condition. The image of the Void, however, expresses an even deeper truth. It reminds us that life is shaped not only by what happens, but also by what does not happen.

The symbol of the prism helps us understand this more clearly.

In a physical prism, white light separates into a spectrum of colors. At first glance the spectrum appears continuous, a ribbon of light flowing from one hue to the next. Yet between the colors there are delicate transitions where one shade dissolves into another. The spectrum is not a solid band but a series of subtle intervals.

The Void may be imagined as one of these intervals—a thin, translucent space between colors. Not black, not gray, but simply clear space, almost like a breath between notes in music.

In Japanese aesthetics there is a word for this kind of meaningful interval: **Ma**. It refers to the space between things—the pause that gives rhythm to music, the open space that allows a painting to breathe, the quiet moment that gives depth to a conversation. Far from being emptiness without value, it is the space that allows form and meaning to emerge.

In much the same way, the Void within the prism of grief is not simply absence. It is the silent space in which life slowly reorganizes itself.

Ancient myths grasped this mysterious relationship between absence and meaning long before psychology gave it a name. One of the most enduring reflections appears in the Greek story of Pandora.

According to the myth, Pandora opened a jar that released every hardship into the world—illness, sorrow, jealousy, struggle. Only when she finally closed the lid did one thing remain inside: hope.

For centuries scholars have debated the meaning of this image. Why was hope left within the jar? Was it preserved for humanity, or withheld from it?

Perhaps the myth suggests something deeper. Hope exists precisely because life contains emptiness. If every desire were fulfilled and every dream realized, hope would no longer be necessary. Desire would fade, and with it the movement that propels human life forward.

The empty spaces in our lives become the vessels of hope.

If the myth of Pandora reveals the cosmic dimension of the Void, sacred tradition offers a more intimate image of how the human heart encounters it.

Among the stories preserved in the Hebrew scriptures, few express this experience more tenderly than the prayer of Hannah. She stood in the sanctuary at Shiloh surrounded by people and still profoundly alone. Others had come to offer gratitude for blessings already received. Hannah carried something different: an emptiness she could not hide.

The Prism of Grief

Her arms had never cradled a child. Her home had never echoed with the laughter she imagined. The cradle of her future remained empty, and that absence weighed upon her heart more heavily than any visible loss.

So she prayed. Her lips moved, yet no sound emerged. Those who watched her misunderstood the depth of her emotion. They could not see that her prayer was not merely a request but the expression of a longing that had lived silently within her for years.

Hannah was not simply asking for a child. She was placing before the Divine the grief of a possibility that had never come to life. In that moment the Void itself became her offering.

The narrative tells that her prayer was finally answered and that a son was born — Samuel. Samuel would become one of the great prophets of Israel, guiding the people at a decisive moment in their history and anointing the first kings of Israel, Saul and David.

Faithful to the promise she had made, Hannah consecrated the child to the Lord and brought him to the temple while he was still very young. The long-awaited son would not become a possession, but an offering.

The most moving part of the story, however, lies even before that fulfillment — in the quiet courage of a human heart willing to bring its emptiness into the presence of the sacred.

Some grief is born not from what life has taken, but from what life never gave.

The Void therefore asks a delicate question of every human life: how shall we live with the spaces that remain unfilled?

One response is bitterness, a constant comparison between the life we inhabit and the one we imagined. Another response is denial, pretending that the abandoned dream never mattered.

There is, however, another possibility.

We may learn to hold the Void without allowing it to eclipse the light that is present.

A fulfilled life is not the one that realized every dream. It is the one that learned to recognize the meaning that still emerges within its limits. The paths we did walk carry their own beauty, even when they differ from those we once imagined.

Every life contains two landscapes: the one we traveled and the one we dreamed. Wisdom lies in honoring both without allowing the second to overshadow the first.

The Void, then, does not have to remain a place of regret. It can become a quiet space of humility, reminding us that life is larger than our plans and richer than our expectations.

Perhaps this is the gentle lesson hidden within it: before grief reveals its deeper mysteries, the soul must first learn to stand peacefully within the spaces where life remained unfinished.

And it is there, in that transparent interval between expectation and reality, that the first hint of light beyond the Void begins to appear—the place where we begin to approach the Veil.

Chapter 12 | The Veil

Death and the Re-signification of Absence

The prism softens into mist.

Death appears to separate what love once held together.

Here the soul must learn that absence is not the end of presence.

If the Thread taught us about attachment and the fear of losing what we love, the Veil confronts us with loss in its most radical form. Here, separation is no longer anticipated; it is embodied. What once trembled with the anxiety of *"What if?"* now stands before the silence of *"What now?"* The Thread stretches no further. We find ourselves before a threshold that seems absolute.

In the spectrum of the prism, there is a point where color dissolves into a soft, translucent mist. This is the Veil. It represents the thinnest of boundaries—the one between the visible and the invisible, the material and the spiritual. For most of our lives, we treat this veil as if it were a wall—a cold and final barrier marking the end of a shared story. However, grief, when faced honestly, teaches us that the veil is not a wall but a horizon. It obscures vision without extinguishing reality.

The central challenge of this facet is the re-signification of absence. When someone dies, the physical world declares them "gone." The chair is empty. The voice is silent. The familiar touch no longer meets our skin. If we remain confined to the testimony of the senses, absence appears total and intolerable. Healing requires a widening of perception. We must learn to see differently—not only with the eyes, but with the interior faculties of memory, conscience, intuition, and love.

This is not a denial of reality; it is an expansion of it. Immortality is not a poetic consolation offered to soften despair, but life itself transformed in its mode of expression. The human heart, however, does not move into this understanding without resistance. Grief inhabits a suspended territory—a space between knowing and not yet integrating.

Modern physics offers a metaphor that captures this peculiar condition. In the thought experiment known as Schrödinger's cat, a cat enclosed within a sealed box is described as being both alive and dead until the box is opened and its condition observed. The paradox lies not in the animal itself, but in the observer's uncertainty. Until the act of seeing occurs, the state appears unresolved.

Grief often lives within such a sealed chamber. The room of the departed remains untouched; the door stays closed. Clothes remain folded precisely as they were, and a book lies open on the bedside table as if awaiting a hand that will never return. A phone number is never deleted; certain streets are avoided; certain restaurants are no longer entered.

As long as the door remains closed and the street is not walked, the psyche maintains a delicate and agonizing suspension. In this stillness, we cling to the illusion that nothing has definitively changed—that somewhere, in a dimension we cannot access, the beloved still inhabits the familiar space.

Nevertheless, the Veil invites us to a higher vantage point. The so-called dead are simply those who have laid aside a dense garment. They have not stepped into a void but into another register of existence. We do not pray for their "rest" as if they were dormant; we commune with their continued journey.

This uncertainty carries both mercy and risk. It softens the brutality of finality and grants the heart time to absorb rupture. But if prolonged indefinitely, it may quietly imprison us in frozen time. We may imagine that by refusing to "open the box" we are preserving love itself. In truth, we may simply be preserving our fear of transformation.

The Veil does not demand abrupt severance. It does not insist on forced closure. It invites maturation. There comes a moment when the room must be entered again, when drawers must be opened, when air must circulate. This act is not betrayal; it is a rite of passage.

Love does not reside in the untouched garment or the sealed drawer. Love resides in the meaning those objects once carried. When we gently alter what was once fixed in time, we are not erasing the beloved—we are allowing love to migrate from form into essence.

The Prism of Grief

Separation produces what may be described as an organic shock—a visceral rupture that reverberates through memory, body, and identity. Even when one holds a spiritual understanding of continuity, the body still registers absence. Longing is not disbelief. It is not weakness of faith. It is love adjusting to altered conditions.

One may know that the soul continues and still weep for the loss of physical proximity. Mourning the form and honoring the essence are not contradictory gestures; they are the two hands of mature love.

If there is an image that clarifies this transition, it is the horizon. When a ship crosses the sea, there comes a moment when it disappears from sight. To those standing on the shore, it seems to vanish. Yet the ship has not fallen into nothingness; it has simply moved beyond the visible line of perception. Its disappearance is relative to the observer, not absolute in reality.

Death resembles this crossing. The beloved has not ceased to exist; they have passed beyond the horizon of our current vision. The Veil is not annihilation; it is a boundary of perception. What feels like extinction is, in truth, a change of vantage point. Grief hurts because we remain on the shore. Healing begins when we understand that existence continues beyond the line our eyes can trace.

In many spiritual and philosophical traditions, this continuity is not metaphor but coherence. Those who cross the Veil do not enter inertia. They continue to think, to learn, and to evolve. They are not extinguished; they are transformed. Relationship remains possible—though its grammar changes.

The thinning or thickening of the Veil is not mechanical; it is vibrational. When despair hardens into revolt, perception narrows. When longing becomes serene—no longer desperate, no longer denying—resonance becomes possible. Our ethical growth becomes shared joy. Our interior peace becomes a bridge.

The most authentic way to love someone beyond the Veil is to live with such clarity and integrity that our own life becomes a signal across the horizon.

Ultimately, the Veil teaches us a new language of love. In other facets of grief, we sought security, identity, and belonging. Here, we are invited to essentiality. We discover that the most vital aspects of a person were never confined to flesh: their kindness, their humor, their moral courage, their way of seeing the world.

You cannot bury a memory that reshaped your character.

You cannot cremate an influence that transformed your conscience.

You cannot seal tenderness inside a coffin.

Love does not end. It changes grammar.

It conjugates itself differently. It no longer arrives through footsteps in the hallway or a familiar voice calling our name. It arrives as quiet strength when we are about to give up. It arrives as memory that warms instead of wounds. It arrives as conscience whispering: *Live well.*

The relationship does not disappear; it deepens its invisibility. What once required touch now requires trust; what once required proximity now requires interiority.

The Prism of Grief

We were never standing before a wall. We were standing before a horizon. And every horizon is only the meeting point between sight and mystery. Beyond it, life continues its vast and luminous navigation.

Yet when the beloved crosses that distant line, something else begins within us. Silence creates echoes. Questions return. Words unsaid surface. The external crossing gives way to an interior journey.

In that inward terrain, grief does not only veil the other—it begins to reveal ourselves.

For when absence is re-signified, another layer of grief emerges. The loss of the other gradually gives way to the encounter with one's own unfinished heart. Silence amplifies memory. Echoes reveal what remained unresolved. Words unspoken return with unexpected force.

Death does not only separate; it exposes.

It brings to light the fragile threads we left tangled—regrets, guilt, apologies withheld, love imperfectly expressed. The horizon we thought was outward now turns inward.

And thus grief changes terrain once more. No longer centered on the one who crossed the Veil, it begins to circle the corridors of our own conscience.

The prism turns inward into a new geometry.

The Labyrinth.

Chapter 13 | The Labyrinth

The Weight of Guilt and the Path of Forgiveness

The prism bends inward into winding corridors.

Memory circles the past in search of what might have been changed.

Here the soul must confront guilt and discover the path of forgiveness.

In the itinerary of the prism, the Labyrinth is the facet where light turns inward and becomes trapped in recursive reflection. Here grief no longer looks toward the horizon or through the Veil; it circles upon itself. When a loss is sudden, tragic, or follows a strained relationship, the mind often retreats from the unbearable weight of the present into the corridors of the past. We pace the endless *"what ifs,"* searching for the precise moment when a different word, a different choice, or a different gesture might have altered the outcome.

The Labyrinth is built from the stones of unfinished business. It is constructed from the relentless rhythm of *"I should have," "I could have,"* and *"Why didn't I?"* These questions are not merely cognitive loops; they are spiritual entanglements. Guilt is often frozen love—a longing to repair what can no longer be repaired in the form we once knew.

Within this terrain we are not only mourning the one who departed; we are mourning our own perceived failure to have been enough for them. The tragedy of the loss is replayed in endless variations within the mind, each repetition an attempt to renegotiate reality.

The mind believes that if it can locate the precise turning point—the unsaid sentence, the missed gesture—it might restore equilibrium. Unfinished business becomes a summons. What remains unresolved exerts gravity. We do not enter the Labyrinth out of curiosity; we are drawn into it by the unfinished threads of love and regret. The more we resist the descent, the stronger its pull becomes. What is not faced does not dissolve—it waits.

At the center of this maze lies a subtle but powerful illusion: the illusion of control.

Guilt is paradoxical. It wounds, yet it comforts. If we convince ourselves that our action—or inaction—caused the catastrophe, then the world still appears governed by understandable rules. If we were responsible, then perhaps everything was preventable.

The alternative is more unsettling: that life unfolds according to a rhythm larger than our will, and that even our deepest love cannot suspend mortality.

We often prefer the burning sting of guilt to the colder ache of helplessness. To admit we could not have saved them, could not have foreseen every turn, could not have held back the tide, is to confront the limits of our humanity. As long as we remain within the territory of *"If only,"* we preserve the illusion that we were sovereign over events.

But this sovereignty is imaginary. It binds us to a shadow dialogue with ourselves rather than to the living memory of the one we lost.

The ancient Greek myth of the Labyrinth offers a symbolic map of this interior struggle. King Minos confined the Minotaur—half man, half beast—within an immense maze so intricate that none who entered could easily return. The structure itself was designed to disorient. Its corridors multiplied, split, and rejoined, mirroring the confusion of those who walked them.

The hero Theseus chose to descend into that structure knowing that confrontation was unavoidable.

The Labyrinth, with its branching paths and repeated turns, reflects our own search through grief. We test explanations. We rehearse conversations. We follow one hypothesis and then another. Trial and error becomes our method. We move down one corridor of memory only to find ourselves returned to the same unresolved chamber.

Each path appears promising, yet none provides release. Through this chain of attempts, we are slowly guided toward the center.

There waits the Minotaur.

In grief, the Minotaur is not death itself. It is the monster that lives within—the relentless voice of self-judgment that declares, *"You failed."* It is the part of us that refuses mercy. It devours peace by feeding on regret.

Theseus did not enter the maze empty-handed. Ariadne, moved by compassion, placed in his palm a fragile thread before he descended. It was simple, easily overlooked—hardly a weapon against a beast. The thread did not prevent him from confronting the monster, nor did it eliminate danger. But it ensured his return.

In our own labyrinth of guilt, that thread is self-forgiveness.

Not indulgence.

Not denial.

But the sober recognition that we acted with the light we possessed at the time. We cannot judge our former selves with the knowledge that only suffering later revealed. To do so is to demand omniscience from a being who was always learning.

The thread is humility. It is the acceptance that love is not measured by perfection, but by sincerity of effort.

Confronting the Minotaur requires courage. Returning requires consciousness. Forgiveness does not erase responsibility; it restores proportion. It reminds us that we are participants in life's unfolding, not its architects.

Across many spiritual traditions, the human journey is understood as woven across time. What feels unfinished is rarely erased; it transforms. The desire to repair does not vanish with death—it seeks new expression.

If words remained unsaid, tenderness withheld, gestures never offered, grief invites us not to remain paralyzed before absence but to redirect love into presence. Every act of kindness performed in the name of the one we lost becomes continuation rather than compensation.

We move from the sterile soil of *"If only"* to the fertile ground of *"From now on."*

This is reparation—not as repayment, but as renewal.

When we believe we failed someone who has crossed the Veil, we often imagine them frozen in disappointment. Yet maturity invites another possibility: that those who see more clearly would not wish us trapped in self-condemnation.

If love continues, then so too does mercy.

The departed do not need our endless punishment; they need our growth.

The Labyrinth begins to loosen when we recognize that guilt is often an inverted form of pride. It assumes we could have controlled what was never ours to command. To relinquish guilt is not to trivialize responsibility. It is simply to differentiate between what was ours and what never was.

Eventually, in the center of the maze, the Minotaur appears less monstrous. Often it reveals itself as a frightened fragment of ourselves—an inner child convinced that catastrophe proves unworthiness. When we offer that fragment compassion instead of condemnation, its claws retract. The beast dissolves into vulnerability.

We follow the thread back, not triumphant but clarified.

The Labyrinth was not a trap; it was an initiation.

It taught us that mercy must be applied inwardly before it can radiate outward, and that love distorted by perfectionism becomes guilt, while love tempered by humility becomes freedom.

As we step out of its corridors, something within us has changed. The architecture of self-condemnation has cracked. The air feels different—lighter, but more intense.

Beyond the maze lies another element entirely.

If the Veil refined perception and the Labyrinth purified conscience, what awaits now is not navigation but combustion.

The prism gathers its light once more.

Ahead stands the Fire.

Chapter 14 | The Fire

Loss as a Sacred Initiation

The prism ignites in living flame.

Grief gathers heat until illusion can no longer endure.

Here the soul is not merely wounded—it is refined.

If the Labyrinth required the courage of forgiveness, the Fire demands something even more interior. It does not ask us to navigate; it asks us to be transformed.

There comes a point in grief when the questions quiet, when guilt loosens its grip, when even longing softens. Yet something profound continues beneath the surface. The loss has already altered the external shape of life; now it begins to alter the internal structure of the soul. The prism concentrates. What was diffused becomes intense. What was scattered gathers heat.

The Prism of Grief

Fire is not merely destruction. It is refinement. It is the element through which form is tested and essence revealed.

In classical alchemical thought, transformation unfolds through stages. First comes dissolution—the breakdown of former structures. What once seemed stable begins to decompose. Identities that appeared coherent reveal their hidden fractures. Certainties melt. The self that existed before the loss cannot remain intact. This collapse feels catastrophic, yet it marks the beginning of reconfiguration.

Then comes clarification. In the wake of breakdown, what is essential begins to separate from what was merely habitual. Illusions thin. Motivations become transparent. The superficial loses weight. Values once taken for granted are reconsidered. Grief sharpens perception. What truly matters stands in relief.

Finally comes integration. Vitality returns—not as the restoration of the former self, but as the emergence of a refined one. Life resumes, though not as it was. Something has shifted irreversibly. The personality reorganizes around deeper priorities. The Spirit moves forward carrying both memory and transformation.

Grief often follows this arc: collapse, clarity, reconfiguration. It does not return us to who we were; it invites us into who we are becoming.

This is not punishment; it is purification.

Grief burns away illusions of permanence. It strips the ego of its quiet presumption—the belief that existence must conform to our expectations. It exposes the hidden assumption that love can secure us against impermanence. In the heat of suffering, what is false cannot endure. Ambitions that once consumed us lose urgency. The need to dominate yields to the need to understand. What survives is not what was loudest, but what was truest.

An ancient image from the Hebrew tradition deepens this metaphor. Moses encounters a bush that burns yet is not consumed. The flame reveals the presence of the Eternal without annihilating the plant itself. Sacred fire, in this narrative, does not destroy essence—it discloses it. Likewise, the moral fire of grief does not extinguish the Spirit; it reveals what in us cannot be consumed.

Yet transformation is not automatic. There is a moment in every interior fire when one is tempted to retreat—to numb, to harden, to close. The flame can purify, but it can also calcify. What determines the outcome is not the intensity of the heat but the willingness to remain present within it. Fire invites surrender, not collapse; participation, not resistance. The posture of the soul matters.

The human being is not a finished structure but a consciousness in development. Every experience—joyful or devastating—imprints itself upon the moral architecture of the self. If received rebelliously, suffering hardens into bitterness. If received reflectively, it deepens into wisdom. Fire does not choose for us; it reveals what we choose.

Metallurgy offers another quiet analogy. Raw metal extracted from the earth contains both substance and impurity. When placed in the furnace, heat does not create value—it reveals it. Under sustained intensity, distortions realign and hidden elements separate. Steel gains resilience not by avoiding fire but by passing through it repeatedly, tempered by cycles of heat and cooling. Without tempering it remains brittle; with tempering it acquires strength that is both firm and flexible.

So too the Spirit: grief, consciously integrated, produces a depth that untouched innocence cannot.

The Phoenix myth expresses this transformation symbolically. In ancient traditions, the Phoenix does not simply burn; it prepares. Near the end of its life cycle, it gathers fragrant branches and constructs a nest. From within that structure, ignition occurs. The fire is not imposed from outside; it arises as part of the rhythm of becoming.

When the flames subside, the Phoenix emerges from its own ashes—not as repetition, but as continuation transformed.

The ashes are not foreign residue; they are the remains of a former identity. Nothing essential is lost, yet nothing returns unchanged. The myth dignifies transformation rather than glorifying destruction. The Phoenix symbolizes individuation—the journey of the self through experience toward greater coherence. Its rebirth is not escape from suffering but evolution through it.

Likewise, the human Spirit does not bypass sorrow. It evolves by passing through it.

Each grief marks a threshold. Something must burn—not the core of being, but the rigidities that confined it. Expectations dissolve. Control relinquishes its throne. Pride yields to perspective. What rises afterward is not invulnerability, but depth.

Within a progressive vision of the Spirit, no experience is wasted. Suffering does not descend as arbitrary punishment; it functions as acceleration. What might have required years of gradual softening is sometimes accomplished in a single encounter with loss. Fire compresses time. It precipitates maturity. It strips away excess so that essence may stand.

What once wounded, when consciously assimilated, becomes discernment. What once destabilized becomes structure.

Fire does not merely refine the individual; it aligns the individual with a broader moral order. What burns away is not only illusion, but resistance to reality. What remains is a self more attuned to the ethical rhythm of existence itself—less reactive, less self-absorbed, more proportionate in its responses. The Spirit begins to resonate with something larger than personal narrative.

This is not an exaltation of suffering; it is an acknowledgment of its formative power. Devastation can become material for reconstruction at another level. The heart, once broken open, does not shrink—it expands its capacity for depth. The one who has faced helplessness understands limits without despair. The one who has relinquished control understands trust without naïveté.

If the Veil revealed continuity beyond death and the Labyrinth restored integrity within conscience, the Fire reveals continuity within the self. We are not shattered by grief; we are reconfigured by it. The ego's dross thins. The Spirit's coherence becomes perceptible. Identity anchors less in circumstance and more in ethical alignment.

When the flames settle, what remains is a self more transparent to itself—freer from illusion, steadier in its interior axis, less vulnerable to trivial agitation. What began as rupture becomes refinement. What began as helplessness becomes humility. What began as loss becomes luminosity.

Fire does not erase grief. It consecrates it.

And what is consecrated does not remain ash. What survives the furnace acquires density—quiet, enduring, radiant. It shines not because it escaped flame, but because it passed through it.

In the crucible of sorrow, something incorruptible begins to take form.

The prism gathers its light once more: from dissolution comes clarity, from clarity integration, and from integration something enduring.

And that enduring substance—refined by fire, tempered by experience, aligned with a larger moral order—begins to take on the quiet incorruptibility of gold.

Chapter 15 | The Gold

Grief Transformed into Compassion

The prism settles into gold.

What has endured the fire becomes quiet strength.

Here grief no longer burns—it illuminates.

In the ancient Sumerian myth of Inanna, the Queen of Heaven chooses to abandon her temples and descend into the Great Below—the underworld of her sister, Ereshkigal. Inanna prepares for this journey by dressing in her most royal finery, wearing a golden crown, a necklace of lapis lazuli, golden rings upon her fingers, and carrying the measuring rod of power as a shield of her status. Yet the laws of the underworld are absolute, and at each of the seven gates the gatekeeper Neti demands a tribute.

At the first gate she must relinquish her crown.

At the second, her beads.

At the third, her golden rings.

Gate by gate, her royal status is peeled away until, by the time she reaches the throne of the Dead, she is naked and bowed low. She is no longer a queen defined by her ornaments; she is a soul reduced to its primary substance.

She dies in that darkness.

Yet when she is eventually resurrected and returns to the upper world, she is different. She still wears the gold, but it no longer defines her power—it signifies her survival. She has moved from the gold of decoration to the gold of distillation.

In the depths of this "Great Below," the soul often asks whether it is being punished. Whether we mourn the death of a beloved companion, the loss of a lifelong vocation, or the erosion of our own health, the first instinct of the ego is to interpret suffering as persecution or cosmic failure. We feel diminished, as though the light of the world has been withdrawn as a verdict against us.

Yet the Gold reveals another possibility.

The descent is not a sentence but an initiation. It is the process through which the Spirit moves from the decoration of virtue—the kindness we display when life is easy—to the distillation of character that emerges only when everything superficial has been removed. Wisdom is not conquered by avoiding darkness; it is discovered when darkness reveals what in us cannot be destroyed.

This distillation is the work of the furnace.

If Fire purified, Gold endures. What has passed through flame does not return unchanged, yet neither does it disappear. Something has been reduced, while something quieter has condensed. The heat has subsided, but its labor remains embedded within the very structure of the soul, transforming what was once intensity into density, what once blazed into a settled and enduring substance.

Gold is not manufactured by fire; it is disclosed by it.

Within raw ore lie both value and impurity, inseparably fused. The furnace does not create worth—it separates it. Under sustained heat, what cannot endure dissolves, leaving behind a cohesive element resistant to corrosion and capable of bearing immense weight without fracturing. Its strength is not rigidity but integrity.

So it is with the human spirit after grief has been consciously endured.

At this stage compassion is no longer merely emotional identification; it becomes structural. The one who has suffered no longer needs to imagine another's pain in order to recognize it. They can hear its tone in a neighbor's silence, trace its outline in restrained speech, or perceive it in the quiet fatigue behind a composed face.

Their presence acquires a particular gravity—not the heaviness of burden, but the groundedness of stability. It becomes an anchor for those still caught in the storm.

Gold does not glitter with the nervous agitation of the ego.

It simply holds warmth.

Loss is not erased; it is illuminated.

This is the soul's version of Kintsugi—the Japanese art of repairing broken pottery with lacquer mixed with powdered gold. The artisan does not attempt to hide the fractures or return the vessel to its original state. To do so would deny its history. Instead, the breakage is revealed and honored. The vessel returns not to its previous form but to a new state of greater value, where the gold becomes the narrative of its endurance.

There is a courageous dignity in showing these seams. The gold that fills them signifies the strength that allowed the soul to remain standing when surrender would have been easier. It represents a history that cannot be replicated, for the patterns of repair are unique to each life.

Our scars become our truest credentials.

When grief is integrated, the seams of our lives are no longer marks of failure but veins of precious metal holding the fragments together. The value of the spirit is no longer measured by original wholeness but by the beauty of its repair.

Grief becomes part of the moral architecture of the self—incorporated rather than exiled. Because it is integrated, it no longer destabilizes identity; it becomes its foundation.

From that foundation emerges a subtle availability: the capacity to remain calm when others tremble, patient when others are undone. Grief becomes service without proclamation—not through dramatic sacrifice but through posture, reliability, and restraint. It is the quiet ability to hold tension without transmitting it.

Gold bends without shattering. It yields without disintegrating.

Likewise, the matured spirit is no longer brittle. Having relinquished the illusion that control guarantees safety, it no longer fears vulnerability in the same way. Strength and tenderness begin to coexist.

Experience redistributes the weight within the self.

Personal suffering ceases to feel like isolated injustice and becomes part of a shared human inheritance. This recognition does not trivialize pain—it contextualizes it. When we perceive the fractures in others, we respond not with pity but with a deep resonance, recognizing the same gold that binds our own soul.

In this recognition resentment loses its oxygen. Hardship is no longer interpreted as persecution but as participation in the common condition of embodied life.

Compassion expands through recognition.

As the ego's excess thins, the frantic need to defend identity weakens. We no longer require constant validation to remain upright. Misunderstanding wounds less deeply; offense loses its immediacy. The interior ground has become more stable.

Gold is called noble not because it is untouchable, but because it does not easily oxidize. In chemistry a noble metal resists the corrosive reactions that degrade others. While many metals tarnish under ordinary exposure, gold remains entirely itself.

So too the spirit refined by grief becomes less reactive to the abrasions of daily life. Having endured the greater fire, the minor sparks of everyday friction—small injustices, irritations, misunderstandings—no longer find sufficient oxygen within the soul to ignite resentment.

It does not harden.

It stabilizes.

This is the hallmark of the integrated self.

It does not retreat into indifference but settles into presence. There is a quiet liberation in this stage. The self is no longer preoccupied with restoring the past or haunted by the ghost of who it once was. It becomes oriented toward coherence in the present.

Ambitions once driven by the need to outrun mortality soften. Desires once frantic become proportionate. The scales shift from acquisition to meaning, from performance to authenticity, from possession to participation.

Life is held differently now.

With the knowledge of how easily the vessel can break, we no longer grip it with a desperate fist; we hold it with an open, steady palm.

This transformation also resolves the crisis of utility encountered earlier in the journey. When the titles of our careers, the security of status, or the vigor of youth are stripped away—much like Inanna's jewels at the gates—we are forced to confront the Spirit who remains beneath these temporary forms.

Here compassion becomes an inward act of justice.

We learn to treat our own limitations with the same patience we extend to others. The soul is no longer punished for its "unproductiveness." Instead, its quiet presence is honored.

When we forgive ourselves for the inevitable incompleteness of our current stage of growth, the authentic voice of our emotions can emerge without condemnation. We no longer suppress our feelings in order to maintain a social mask. Instead we listen to them with the attentiveness of a wise parent.

This tenderness toward ourselves soon extends outward.

Service ceases to be a performance of virtue and becomes a spontaneous movement of the soul. We no longer help others to prove our worth; we help because we recognize our shared fragility.

Compassion becomes durable.

It does not rely on emotional intensity but expresses itself through consistency, patience, and reliability. Gold does not proclaim its value; it simply remains. And in remaining it becomes a refuge.

Others sense this interior climate—not as brilliance or superiority but as safety. There is less volatility, less abruptness, less need to dominate space.

Warmth replaces glare.

Pain that once threatened to fragment identity has reorganized it. What began as destabilization has become orientation; what began as burning has become cohesion. The self becomes less impressed by spectacle and more attentive to substance, less reactive to turbulence and more attuned to proportion.

The Prism of Grief

Gold remembers the fire, but it is no longer the flame.

Grief is no longer an adversary. It becomes part of the biography of the soul. It has left marks—but those marks are not wounds that reopen; they are the seams that hold.

The spirit now stands differently in the world—not invulnerable, not immune to future loss, but less easily undone. Less startled by impermanence. More capable of remaining present without collapsing into despair.

What survives the furnace acquires density—quiet, enduring, luminous. It shines not because it escaped suffering, but because it passed through it without dissolving into bitterness.

This is not conquest.

It is consolidation.

The self has not overcome grief; it has incorporated it. It carries memory without corrosion, loss without fragmentation, tenderness without fragility.

Because the gold now fills the fractures, the light of the world no longer passes through the soul unchanged. It strikes the seams, catches the edges of repair, and refracts into new colors.

From this enduring substance the prism prepares its final movement—the reunion of color and clarity, where grief, once dispersed across many facets, gathers again into a single, integrated light.

Chapter 16 | The Reintegrated Light

Finding Luminous Coherence

In ancient stories, Iris was the goddess of the rainbow, a winged messenger who moved between the heights of Olympus and the depths of the human world. She did not represent the sun alone, nor the storm alone, but the shimmering bridge created when the two met. She was the proof that the light of the heavens could touch the soil of the earth without losing its divinity. To walk the path of Iris is to understand that the rainbow is not a fracture of the sky, but its most complete expression.

We conclude our itinerary where we began: with the mystery of the light. We started this journey as a single, simple beam—a breath of the Creator, a luminous seed that carried vast potentiality but little self-awareness. At that entrance, we did not value the light because we had never known the shadow. We were a cocoon of possibilities, a seed tucked safely away, waiting for the resistance of the world to force our metamorphosis.

After traveling through the blue of childhood, the red of desire, the dark of depression, and the gold of service, we arrive at the state of the Reintegrated Light. In the physical world, there is a phenomenon known as Newton's Disc. When a circle painted with all the colors of the spectrum is spun at high speed, the individual hues—the reds, the violets, the greens—suddenly vanish. They do not disappear into nothingness; they melt back into a pure, brilliant white.

In the landscape of the soul, this is the state of Inner Maturity. It is a peace that does not come from the absence of conflict, but from the harmonious integration of all the shades of our lived experience. As the ancient sage Lao Tzu observed, a journey of a thousand miles begins with a single step. This plenitude is not reached by a sudden leap, but by the quiet courage of persistence—the decision to keep walking through the different hues of life until they begin to merge.

If one is willing to take that step now, even while feeling fractured, they soon find they are joining a silent, magnificent procession of people who have navigated these same facets of pain. These are the individuals who have chosen to stand tall, even with their cracks. They do not hide their history; they irradiate a singular light from within—a light refined by the very hardships that threatened to extinguish it. By learning to love oneself, including every wounded part of that history, the person becomes a beacon for others, proving that the repair is often more beautiful than the original vessel.

The final teaching of the prism is a sober, radiant truth: grief never truly disappears; it evolves. The pain that once blinded now gives way to a profound depth perception. The world appears more clearly because its shadows have been mapped, and love is felt more deeply because its transience is understood. At this final threshold, there is a realization of the supreme victory of the self: love is independent of form. Throughout this journey, there was a struggle as the "envelope" of life changed—when the body failed, the job ended, or the person departed. However, in the Reintegrated Light, these are seen as temporary containers for an eternal essence. This is the peace of the traveler who has crossed the mountain range and can now look back at the peaks and the valleys with equal gratitude, seeing finally that the dark facet was as necessary as the gold. Without the descent, the seed would never have found the strength to break its shell and reach for the sun.

This transformation is the knighting of the soul by the very sword of its sorrow. To have faced the darkness and refused to let it harden the heart is the highest achievement of a human being. It is the arrival at a state of luminous coherence, where the voice of the emotions is finally heard and integrated. One no longer fears the spectrum because they *are* the spectrum.

The great illusion of the human experience is that loss breaks a life. We feel fractured, diminished, and incomplete. But at the end of this journey, looking back at the Prism of Grief, the truth is revealed: the prism does not break the light; it reveals what the light already contains. White light appears simple until it hits the glass; only then do the hidden blues, the secret reds, and the buried golds come to the surface. In the same way, a life without loss might appear whole, but it remains unrevealed. Its talents remain hidden; its divinity remains a theory. It is only when love encounters the resistance of death, change, and time that the true complexity and beauty of character are made visible. Grief did not take the light away; it forced the light to show its true colors. What was once seen as brokenness is now understood as expansion.

Before we step back into the world, let us carry with us the wisdom of the wind.

There is an ancient story of an Oak and a Reed that grew side by side, illustrating the final lesson of our journey: the strength of fluidity. The Oak was magnificent, its trunk thick and its branches unyielding. It took pride in its "stubbornness," planting its roots with a strictness that defied the elements. To the observer, the Oak represents the "stiffness of the ego"—that part of us that believes survival depends on remaining unchanged. When the mild breezes blew, the Oak stood motionless, mocking the slender Reed that bowed and trembled at every puff of air.

But then came the Great Storm—the kind of grief that tests the very architecture of existence. The Oak, trusting in its rigidity, refused to move. It met the violence of the wind with the full force of its pride, until the tension became unbearable and its mighty heartwood snapped. The Oak fell, not because it was weak, but because it could not bend.

The Reed, nevertheless, survived. It represents the "flexibility of the Spirit," which does not survive by being "stronger" than the wind, but by being more "truthful" to it. The Reed recognized the exigencies of the moment; it yielded, it conformed to the curve of the gale, and it allowed itself to be momentarily swept low. To the observer, it appeared defeated, even subjugated. But as the storm passed, the Reed simply stood tall again.

It remained part of the landscape, rooted deeply in the soil of its own humility, ready to enjoy the returning hues of light that compose one day after the next.

We often mistake rigidity for strength and vulnerability for weakness. But the Reintegrated Light teaches us that true resilience is the ability to flow with the "transcendental itinerary" of life. Like the Reed, we do not need to be unbreakable; we only need to be unshakeable in our essence. By bending to the sorrows of the world without letting them harden us, we prove that virtues, even when quiet and unseen, are the strongest roots of all.

You are not the Oak, shattered by the weight of what you could not control. You are the Reed—alive, enduring, and forever bathed in the shimmering bridge of the rainbow.

The journey through the prism is complete. The colors have been seen, the myths have been lived, and the thread has been loosened. One steps out of these chapters and back into the world, not to find the light, but to be it. For in the heart of the Reintegrated Light, there is no more separation—only the infinite, vibrant, and eternal presence of love.

Take a moment now to look at your own life through the prism. Do not look for what is missing; acknowledge what has been uncovered. Your tears testified to your capacity for depth. Your guilt betrayed your secret desire for goodness. Your service manifested your own divinity.

You are the light.

You have always been the light.

The prism simply helped you see it.

The Prism of Grief

You entered carrying a light
so small you did not notice it.
You thought it was breath,
or memory,
or simply the quiet pulse of being alive.
Then the glass appeared.
The light touched the prism,
and suddenly the sky broke open —
blue longing,
red fire,
gold hidden in the bones of sorrow.
You said:
"I am broken."
But the light said:
"No.
I am only showing you
what you are made of."
You walked through shadows
where love wore the mask of absence.
You crossed corridors
where the heart asked questions
no voice could answer.
Still the light did not leave.
It hid in your tears.

Jussara Pretti Korngold

It waited in the ashes.
It whispered beneath the silence of loss.
Until one morning,
without announcement,
the colors returned to one another.
Not erased.
Transformed.
Now the light moves quietly within you —
no longer afraid of the glass,
no longer divided by the spectrum.
And if you listen closely,
you may hear what it has been saying
since the beginning:
You were never shattered.
You were becoming.

Recommended Path for Further Study

Foundations of Spiritist Philosophy

- **Kardec, Allan.** *The Spirits' Book*. The foundational pillar of Spiritist doctrine, essential for understanding the immortality of the Spirit. *(Published by the United States Spiritist Federation in partnership with the International Spiritist Council).*
- **Kardec, Allan.** *The Gospel According to Spiritism*. A profound guide to the moral transformation required to find peace amidst suffering. *(Published by the United States Spiritist Federation in partnership with the International Spiritist Council).*
- **Kardec, Allan.** *Heaven and Hell*. Offers a rational perspective on the transition between planes of existence and the law of cause and effect. *(Published by the United States Spiritist Federation in partnership with the International Spiritist Council).*
- **Kardec, Allan.** *The Mediums' Book*. For those seeking to understand the mechanics of communication between the physical and spiritual dimensions. *(Published by the United States Spiritist Federation in partnership with the International Spiritist Council).*
- **Xavier, Francisco Cândido (Spirit: André Luiz).** *Our Home (Nosso Lar)*. A vivid account of life in the spiritual world and the continuity of service.

- **Xavier, Francisco Cândido (Spirit: André Luiz).** *Evolution in Two Worlds.* A technical yet comforting study on the interaction between the Spirit and biological life.

The Psychological Series of Joanna de Ângelis

- **de Ângelis, Joanna (Spirit) / Franco, Divaldo.** *Plenitude.* An essential text for finding transcendental meaning in life's most difficult transitions. *(Published by Leal Publisher).*
- **de Ângelis, Joanna / Franco, Divaldo.** *Self-Discovery: An Inner Search.* A masterful guide for navigating the journey from the ego to the Spirit. *(Published by Leal Publisher).*
- **de Ângelis, Joanna / Franco, Divaldo.** *The Integral Human Being.* Bridges the gap between modern psychology and the eternal nature of the soul. *(Published by Leal Publisher).*

- **de Ângelis, Joanna / Franco, Divaldo.** *Existential Conflicts.* Provides deep insights into the shadows and fears that cloud our inner light. *(Published by Leal Publisher).*
- **de Ângelis, Joanna / Franco, Divaldo.** *The Awakening of the Spirit.* Focuses on the process of maturation that allows the soul to claim its divine inheritance. *(Published by Leal Publisher).*
- **de Ângelis, Joanna / Franco, Divaldo.** *Times of Health and Consciousness.* Explores the profound relationship between psychological balance and spiritual health. *(Published by Leal Publisher).*

Analytical Psychology, Mythology, & Meaning

- **Jung, Carl G.** *The Archetypes and the Collective*

Unconscious. A gateway to understanding the universal symbols—like the Shadow and the Persona—that appear in our crises.

- **Jung, Carl G.** *Modern Man in Search of a Soul.* A foundational work on the "afternoon of life" and the shift from worldly ambition to spiritual meaning.
- **Frankl, Viktor E.** *Man's Search for Meaning.* Written from the depths of suffering, this work proves that meaning is our greatest anchor.
- **Campbell, Joseph.** *The Hero with a Thousand Faces.* Frames personal grief as part of the universal "Hero's Journey" leading toward a deeper life.
- **Hillman, James.** *The Force of Character: And the Lasting Life.* A poetic look at how aging and loss are the final shaping of our true character.
- **Hollis, James.** *Finding Meaning in the Second Half of Life.* A compassionate guide for those facing the "middle passage" of identity loss.
- **Yanagi, Soetsu.** *The Unknown Craftsman.* Provides the philosophical heart behind the Kintsugi metaphor and the beauty of the imperfect.

About the Author

Jussara Korngold is an internationally recognized author, educator, and leader at the intersection of spiritual philosophy and humanitarian service. For over thirty years, she has balanced a rigorous professional life in finance and philanthropy with a profound commitment to the study and practice of Spiritist teachings and the evolution of the Spirit.

A polyglot fluent in four languages, Jussara serves in executive leadership roles within international not-for-profit organizations, contributing both strategically and financially to initiatives dedicated to social transformation. Over the past two decades, she has been a central figure in the Spiritist movement in the United States, serving in key executive and leadership capacities.

Her philanthropic work has been recognized by Vogue, and she was featured in New York Magazine's "Fifty Faces of New York's Religious Plurality" as a prominent spiritual voice in New York City and beyond.

A prolific author and translator, Jussara has edited over 70 volumes and is a guest instructor at the Menla Institute. Her literary contributions to the study of the soul span decades, including Those Left Behind (2006), Eternal Voices (2011), and Inner Transformation (2020), as well as her recent exploration of the afterlife, Transcendence (2024).

She is also co-host of the Psychology and Spirituality podcast, where she explores the convergence between analytical psychology and the immortal nature of the human spirit. Through her work, she continues to build bridges between cultures, traditions, and fields of knowledge, offering language for the deepest transitions of the human experience.

LAB EDITORIAL

www.ingramcontent.com/pod-product-compliance
Lightning Source LLC
LaVergne TN
LVHW010102110826
845155LV00028B/456

* 9 7 8 1 9 4 8 1 0 9 4 9 9 *